Kim's Quest

Kim's Quest

5-day holiday programme for 5-12s

Teaching materials, crafts, outside games, daily programme outlines, budgeting guides, handout materials, all–age worship format, video recommendations, and more...

Mark Griffiths

MONARCH
BOOKS

Oxford, UK, & Grand Rapids, Michigan

First published in the UK in 2004 by Monarch Books
(a publishing imprint of Lion Hudson plc),
Mayfield House, 256 Banbury Road, Oxford OX2 7DH
Tel: +44 (0) 1865 302750 Fax: +44 (0) 1865 302757
Email: monarch@lionhudson.com
www.lionhudson.com

Illustrations by Doreen Lang

UK ISBN: 1 85424 648 8
US ISBN: 0 8254 6058 1

Distributed by:
UK: Marston Book Services Ltd, PO Box 269,
Abingdon, Oxon OX14 4YN;
USA: Kregel Publications, PO Box 2607,
Grand Rapids, Michigan 49501.

Unless otherwise stated, all biblical quotations are from
the Contemporary English Version, © American Bible Society
1991, 1992, 1995. Used by permission.
Anglicised version © British & Foreign Bible Society 1996.
All rights reserved.

British Library Cataloguing Data
A catalogue record for this book is available
from the British Library.

Book design and production for the publishers by
Gazelle Creative Productions Ltd,
Concorde House, Grenville Place, Mill Hill, London NW7 3SA.
Printed in Malta.

CONTENTS

Choosing videos

How to watch. Where to watch. What to watch.

Ideas for outside games

Outside games and alternatives

Afternoon activities

Why and what afternoon activities?

Format for all—age worship service

All-age worship service format

Appendices

A FEW WORDS FROM THE AUTHOR

- Twelve out of thirteen children in our communities have no contact with church or church groups.
- Parents are desperate to find wholesome, enjoyable and fun activities for their children during what appears to be the ever-increasing school holidays.

How can we look at these two facts and not be excited by the opportunities?

I recently heard Mark Stibbe, the vicar of St Andrew's Church, Chorleywood, teaching on the nativity narrative and particularly the part played by the shepherds. He sees within it the interesting fact that God transformed these shepherds from those who cared for sheep to those who proclaimed far and wide the good news of Christ's birth. He made the prophetic statement that God was equipping our pastors to proclaim the gospel. What interested me further was the fact that Mark felt God wanted to do this now because of the needs of this generation.

Many denominations are encountering the same issues. Simply caring for our sheep – valuable and important as that is – is not enough. God has called us during a time of apparent church decline (certainly in Europe) to become apostolic again; to fill our churches with those who have never heard the gospel message, and more than that to proclaim that same gospel where they are.

Our work with children must be part of God's overall vision for the church, a vision of reaching out and making the gospel accessible to those who have never heard it. Children's ministry allows us access into homes that would otherwise be closed to the gospel message. If we don't reach the younger generations, the average age of congregations will continue to rise and church membership will eventually die away. God's plan for this country is surely not a combination of empty church buildings and ministers "managing decline". God's plan is for a vibrant and healthy church. Children aid this process; they stand as a testimony to new life.

This is holiday club material (or playscheme material, whichever title you prefer) that exists primarily for first contact with those who have never set foot in church. Those who have been brought up in Christian homes or who regularly attend a Christian children's club will also enjoy it and learn much from it, but it was written for a first contact situation and I would encourage you to use it in this context.

Mark Griffiths

WHAT IS A HOLIDAY PLAYSCHEME OR HOLIDAY CLUB?

This may seem a ridiculous question; you will find it far more important than you think. The people of your locality will already have a preconception of what is meant by "holiday playscheme" or "holiday children's club". To present something that is contrary to that preconception is not always easy.

First, we must be clear in our own mind: what are we aiming to do? What is the week for? There are several aims:

1. To encourage Christian children and give them time for praise, prayer and biblical input.
2. To be an evangelistic project geared to reaching children in the local community for Jesus.
3. To be a community-based programme with fun and games and little or no Christian input, but which builds awareness of your church and plants trust for future events in the hearts of those who attend or send their children.

All are perfectly legitimate aims. However, to try and do all three in the one week in the same place at the same time would be an incredible achievement, bordering on impossible. This material was written to fulfil aim 2, but will work perfectly well for all the above. If you are seeking to build up Christian boys and girls then spend more time on the prayer, praise and worship elements and emphasise strongly the Bible lessons and Bible texts. If you are seeking to outwork a community-based programme with little Christian input then concentrate on telling the "Kim's Quest" story and avoid prayer and praise sections.

If you are aiming to bring a Christian message to the children of your community you must be upfront with this. If the activity is taking place in your church then a reasonable person could be expected to conclude that it is Christian in nature (it's worth remembering that we don't always deal with reasonable people!). However, if it is taking place in the church hall which has a reputation for being used by many different groups, or is being held in a local community centre or school, it is important that your advertising mentions clearly your intention to have Christian content. The situation where we attract people to our events by promising one thing and then doing something completely different (a basis on which so many evangelistic initiatives fail) is not the best starting point for introducing people to a God of truth and light.

When we operate this way, we gain respect; openness and honesty always do. Council officials who have come to take a look at projects we have run have never been surprised by the Christian content. They were expecting it. One council representative who came to view one of our playschemes described the praise and worship as exciting and uplifting – not a bad response from someone with no church affiliation.

The gospel is not something strange or embarrassing; it is not something we have to camouflage or hide, and it is something we are very much unashamed of. Some people will be upset by it, but for some it will be the power of God for salvation.

This book contains a day-to-day schedule for running an engaging and potentially life-changing holiday club week.

HOW MUCH SHOULD WE CHARGE?

The cart has arrived before the horse again! The first question is: How much will it cost? The following table will help you:

EXPENDITURE		
Hire of hall	£	If you own the building you may still want to budget for lighting and heating.
Advertising	£	If it is for your church children, it may be a case of photocopies only; if it is for your community, you may need to consider printing charges.
Equipment	£	Do you already have what you need or do you need some extra footballs, tennis rackets, etc? Do you want to buy a large item, e.g. bouncy castle, and allow the playscheme income to pay for it?
Staff costs	£	Are all your staff volunteers or have you employed some people for the week? Do you have volunteers' expenses to think about?
Transport	£	Do you have a church minibus? Then consider fuel costs. Do you need to hire a vehicle?
Outings	£	Are you going to take the children out? If so, taking them to walk in the woods will be free; going to the local pool will cost.
Activity/Materials	£	This is the money needed for craft materials, etc.
Administration	£	Do you need to build in a cost for the time needed to put the whole project together, or is this simply part of the overall mission of the church?
Insurance	£	Definitely worth checking your level of public liability cover and contents cover. Also check if it covers you for outside activities, particularly bouncy castles.
Miscellaneous	£	Backdrops, T-shirts for sale, tuck shop, prizes, etc.
TOTAL	£	

Now you have an expenditure figure. You know what this is going to cost. There are still extra factors affecting what the children have to pay, but they form the income part of the equation.

INCOME		
Budget	£	Did the church council allocate a budget for this event from your overall children's budget allocated by the church? If you are thinking, "What budget?", then I suspect the answer is "No".
Grants	£	Did the local authority give you a grant towards this project? Perhaps you should have asked?
TOTAL	£	

Expenditure minus income will leave you with the actual cost. Now divide the actual cost by the number of children you are expecting (be very realistic at this point, and although faith is a wonderful thing it is often wise to budget against the worst-case scenario).

Expenditure	£	
Income	£	
Actual Cost	£	Expenditure minus income
Numbers expected		
COST PER CHILD	£	Actual cost divided by numbers expected to come

DAILY FORMAT

The daily format is flexible and can be as long or as short as you like. The basic format looks like this:

Full programme (8:30am – 5:45pm)

8:30 – 10:00am	Drop-off and free play
10:00 – 11:00am	TEACHING TIME
11:00 – 11:15am	Biscuit and juice
11:15 – 12:00 noon	Outside games
12:00 – 12:45pm	VIDEO TIME
12:45 – 1:15pm	Lunch (children bring a packed lunch)
1:15 – 2:00pm	CRAFT TIME
2:00 – 4:00pm	Afternoon activities
4:00 – 4:15pm	Biscuit and juice
4:30 – 5:45pm	Collections and free play

Working parents will buy into this, as they can drop their children off before work and collect them after work. It also allows other children to arrive shortly before 10am and leave at 4pm without missing any programmed activities. Free play involves free choice of play items; for this purpose the project will need plenty of computers, board games, TV and video areas, etc.

Full programme without provision for working parents (9:45am – 4:00pm)

9:45am	Arrival
10:00 – 11:00am	TEACHING TIME
11:00 – 11:15am	Biscuit and juice
11:15 – 12:00 noon	Outside games
12:00 – 12:45pm	VIDEO TIME
12:45 – 1:15pm	Lunch (children bring a packed lunch)
1:15 – 2:00pm	CRAFT TIME
2:00 – 4:00pm	Afternoon activities
4:00pm	End

Condensed programme (10am – 12 noon)

10am	Arrival
10:00 – 11:00am	TEACHING TIME

11:00 – 11:15am	Biscuit and juice
11:15 – 12:00 noon	CRAFT TIME
12 noon	End

The advantage here is that, because of the time period (two hours), the project can run every holiday and still not need to register. It is within the time period stated in the 1989 Children's Act for registration.

Personal choice

The timetable you choose is really down to personal choice and community need. It is my view that the full programme, which does not exclude working parents and allows time to have fun with the children in outside-activity environments, is preferable.

For larger projects

If the project has more than 40 children, it is recommended that the group remains in the three teams that they were separated into for teaching time (see notes on set-up and structure under "The Nuts and Bolts"). The teams can then visit the craft, outside games and video areas at different times, for example:

	Blue Team	Red Team	Yellow Team
11:15am to 12 noon	Video	Outside Games	Craft
12 noon to 12:45pm	Craft	Video	Outside Games
1:15pm to 2:00pm	Outside Games	Craft	Video

LEGAL ISSUES AND REGISTRATION

The 1989 Children's Act states that if an activity runs for more than two hours a week and for more than five days a year it must be registered – formerly with social services, now with OFSTED. It is important that our clubs are safe places; where it is possible to police-check our staff, we should do so. However, there are many difficulties in registering: there will need to be one toilet for every eight children, some of our older buildings will need renovation, there is a fee which is payable annually, and the big difficulty is that the majority of staff will need a "play work" qualification.

If you intend to run only one holiday club each year that lasts for five days or less, you do not need to register. I am very keen to point out that this does not allow us to become slack with the requirements; we must do all we can to meet the requirements even if we are not registering. This is particularly true regarding police checks. All your staff should be police-checked as a matter of routine.

REGISTRATION FORM

This form must be completed before your child attends one of our activities.

Child's Name: _____

Address: _____

_____

_____

Telephone Number: _____ D.o.B: _____

Secondary Contact Number: _____

School Attended: _____

Medical Conditions/Food Allergies we should be aware

of: _____

_____

In the event of a major accident, your child will be taken, by ambulance if possible, to the nearest casualty department and parents will be informed as soon as possible. If this is not the procedure you would like us to follow for your child, please notify us in writing.

Signed: _____ Date: _____

_____

Office Use: Team Colour: _____

If you intend to run more than one holiday club, to run for more than two hours a day, and to cater for children under eight years old, then you must contact the Early Years and Child Development Partnership at your local council offices in order to register. Failure to register would constitute a criminal act.

It is also very important that before each child begins the holiday week, he or she should complete a registration form. The registration form should contain at least the information shown on the sample.

There are implications under the Data Protection Act here; you should contact the address given below for further information before you start storing names and addresses either manually or on computer.

There are other items that can be added to the form, such as doctor's name and surgery address.

Legislation surrounding children's clubs and the very serious issues associated with child protection are outside the remit of this book. The rules change with infuriating frequency; the procedure to ensure your club/project has the proper policies in place can be a minefield. The best I can do is point you in the direction of the experts.

For all you need to know about writing a clear child-protection policy, contact:

Churches' Child Protection Advisory Service
PO Box 133, Swanley, Kent, BR8 7UQ
Tel: (0845) 120 45 50

For help on other legal issues, including police checks, contact:

Criminal Records Bureau
Disclosure Services, PO Box 110, Liverpool, L3 6ZZ
Tel: (0870) 90 90 844

For help with data protection issues, contact:

Information Services
Data Protection Registrar, Wycliffe House,
Water Lane, Wilmslow, SK9 5AF
Tel: (01625) 545 745

THE NUTS AND BOLTS

1. Arrival

Arrival and departure are important. Have a good register that keeps track of names, addresses and any ailments that you should be aware of. Have a contact number for parents. Talk to parents; allow them to see your face. It's hard for a parent to trust an anonymous name on the bottom of a sheet of paper. It's much easier to trust someone they've seen and met.

Charge a small admission fee. The more self-sufficient the club can be, the better. Remember: I am suggesting that these clubs can be the seeds for new churches. Some will need to be completely self-sufficient.

2. What's important

It is enough for now to stress that the things that are important to us must be incorporated into the way we run. Here are some principles that I hold as important:

- Children will only listen to you if you listen to them.
- Children will only listen to you if you will have fun with them.
- Children will only listen to you if they like you.
- Children are individuals and like different things.

I believe in these principles, therefore I would not consider running the play scheme without some free-play opportunities. Have a range of activities at the start and finish that the children can choose to do, for example, face-painting, computer games (some children like computers), pool/snooker, coffee bar area (if children will only listen to you if you listen to them, then create a place where they can talk to you – a coffee bar) and craft area (some children like crafts). Don't be so naive as to think that all the children will like everything.

3. Hall set-up and structure

Registration and Tuck Shop		
Blue Team	**Red Team**	**Yellow Team**
A		B
Stage Area		
OHP and Video		**Score Board**

Why three teams?

If two teams are used, then usually there is a winning team and a losing team. Having three teams allows one team to win and the others to come joint second. It allows an element of healthy competitiveness without there needing to be a loser. Other children's groups (some very large groups) work with two teams, one of boys and the other of girls. There are two main disadvantages to this system:

1. There is very rarely an equal mix of boys and girls.
2. It leads to unnecessary tension between the teams and also with social services, who will frown on the practice. (Wherever possible it will pay you to keep government organisations positively inclined towards your work – Jesus had favour with God *and men*.)

4. Staffing

Registration   Three team members should be responsible for registration. This is where you meet the parents. This is the initial contact point. First impressions do last, so put some of your best people here. The registration people will also need to be armed with information regarding trips, etc. This is your public relations department.

Team leaders	There will need to be a sprinkling of leaders in each team. Problems should not be dealt with from the front but sorted quickly from within the team. For the staff as well as for the children it will be a process of education.
Scorekeeper	A competent and upbeat member of the team is needed who will periodically announce the scores.
Technical support	A person who can operate PA systems, videos, OHPs, etc. is invaluable. If done well, this will help you greatly. If done badly, this can destroy your programme.
Front people	Two front people will be responsible for illustrations. If you work with two front people who know what they are doing and have obvious communication gifts, then introduce a third person who can develop and learn. As they come to maturity in this gift, release more responsibility to them. This is a continuous process which allows you to move or sow out into other children's works. The choice of the third person is very important. He or she may not be particularly gifted, but must be humble and teachable and have the heart of a servant. Don't choose anyone without these qualifications.
Others	If you run crafts as part of your programme, then you will need artistic people. A qualified first-aider should not be overlooked. Members of the team will also need to be involved in the visitation programme.

5. And the most important part

What happens after the playscheme is very important; on the final evening give the children invitations to two separate activities:

- **Your weekly children's club.** Don't allow a week's investment to be wasted.

- **An all-age worship service for the whole family that Sunday.** Make the invitation a colouring competition also (see handouts in Appendix 1) and award a prize on that Sunday for the best entry. Make it clear that children must come with their families on that day. This is the starting point for reaching the wider family. During this service, leaflets advertising the Alpha Course (or equivalent) should be readily available.

Teaching Materials

THE PROGRAMME FROM BEGINNING TO END

Welcome (3 minutes)

This is a chance to welcome the children, but also an opportunity to have fun with them. Remember, if you will not have fun with them, they will not listen to you. I prefer to lead the programme with two people at the front. This allows for comical banter between the two. Think differently! Have the two leaders dressed as Barney Rubble™ and Fred Flintstone™ to walk on and welcome the children. Be creative!

Rules (2 minutes)

If there are no clear rules, then the children have no discipline guidelines. They cannot be reprimanded for not obeying rules that they have never heard. Only two simple rules are necessary:

- Nobody leaves their seat. If a child needs to go to the toilet, he or she must put a hand up and ask permission from a leader to go.
- When the whistle blows, everyone stops speaking, sits down, focuses on the front and makes no sound. If you are uncomfortable with the use of a whistle, you can use a horn, or a special word.

These two simple rules will keep everything controlled. Children feel safer and more secure in a disciplined atmosphere.

There must be a method of enforcing the rules. We use the following twofold system:

Positive enforcement
If a team are particularly good (e.g. they sit well, listen well, cheer the loudest, or win a game), they get to roll dice. The score from the dice is added to their overall score. The team with the most points at the end of the week get the biggest prizes; the other teams receive smaller prizes.

Negative enforcement

If a child talks after the whistle has gone or is not sitting and facing the front, their team instantly lose six points.

Prayer (5 minutes)

This can be divided into two sections:

Giving thanks

Children who have prayed for something the day before (or several days before) and whose prayers have been answered should be asked to come and tell the others about it.

Bringing needs

Some of the children will want to pray for certain things. Allow them to come and mention what they are praying for, and ask God together to answer prayer.

Remember, when children have prayers answered they need to be invited to the front so that everyone can give God thanks.

Praise (7 minutes)

This involves singing some lively songs. There are two slots for praise. Make sure you use the first slot for songs they know which contain lots of actions. New songs can be introduced in the second section. Some of the children may not enjoy singing – award six points for the best team singing; suddenly you'll find they enjoy it a lot more!

Game 1 (5 minutes)

Games differ from day to day. But the following points are important:

- In order to play a game they must answer a question on the lesson from the day before.
- Choose one person from each team and then allow that person to choose the rest of the team.
- For games which mention point A and point B, see the hall plan under "The Nuts and Bolts".
- Give points for the teams that cheer people the loudest.
- Play music while the game runs – live music, if possible.
- The first team to complete the game must sit down.

Praise (10 minutes)

The second praise slot is longer, with several songs being used together. Encourage banners, streamers, dancing, etc. Allow some of the children to form a praise group that stands with a microphone to lead the others. I have included a list of good CDs for children in Appendix 4.

Fun Item 1 (5 minutes)

We use several fun items to enhance the programme. You can be creative with your ideas, but we recommend the following:

Guess The Leader
We reveal an interesting fact regarding one of the leaders, for example, "This leader used to live in Spain". Then four leaders are chosen who all try and convince the children that they used to live in Spain. The children then have to guess the leader who was telling the truth. A variation on this theme is to show a picture of the leader as a baby; the leaders all have to try and convince the children that they are the person in the picture.

Strip Search
Here is an idea from Saturday morning television that will help with getting to know the children or leaders. Play some background music. Invite a leader (or a child) to sit in a seat at the front. Then for one minute ask the leader questions such as "Awake or asleep?" The leader will then answer by telling you whether they prefer to be awake or asleep. These are some samples, but there are many more that can be used:

- "Awake or asleep?"
- "Music or reading?"
- "Chocolate or fruit?"
- "Will or Gareth?"

The children/leader will then choose one each time.

Buy It or Bin It
This is a chance for music and video reviews. Ask the children to bring in the videos they watch and the music they listen to. It may not seem overtly Christian, but it is incredibly educational! Form a panel of three (one leader and two children) and allow them to view three videos/CDs for 30 seconds each. Then ask them

whether they would buy them or bin them, and why. Periodically introduce Christian music. This teaches the children critical thought, which is very important for their development.

Who Wants To Be A Chocoholic?
This is based on the television game show *Who Wants to Be A Millionaire?* A child is chosen from the audience. They are asked questions in increasing degrees of difficulty. They are given four answers to the questions and have to choose the right one. For a right answer they gain more chocolate; for a wrong answer they lose it all. The trick is to know when to quit and take the chocolate. The children have lifelines: they can ask the audience or a leader the answer to a question.

Aerobics Workout
A piece of music is played and the children copy the leader at the front performing their aerobic workout.

This slot can also be used for all sorts of fun items such as puppet skits, etc. Use it to have fun with the children.

Game 2 (5 minutes)

Make sure that the people who take part in game 2 are different from those who were involved in game 1.

Fun item 2 (5 minutes)

Other items may be added to the first section, such as video clips of an outing, interviews with community members, etc. Use your imagination.

Bible text (3 minutes)

We display the memory verse on the OHP from the start of preaching time and refer to it frequently, but you may prefer to encourage the children to memorise the text. There are many ways to teach a Bible text. A few ideas are given below, but there are literally hundreds of possibilities. Be creative.

- Write the Bible text on balloons and burst a balloon as each word of the verse is read.
- Make the verse into a jigsaw puzzle.

- Write the verse on an object which communicates its message, e.g. "You are a light to my path" can be written on a lamp or a drawing of a bulb.
- "The Lord is my shepherd" can be written on five cut-out sheep.

Remember that memorisation of the verse is not as important as understanding. Children may win a prize if they can quote "The Lord is my shepherd", but their lives will be changed if they understand it.

Copies of each of the Bible texts are included in Appendix 3 for you to photocopy onto acetate.

Announcements (2 minutes)

Summer camps, special events, your regular weekly outreach club, all-age service, etc. all need mentioning here. If you are going to announce birthdays, you must be consistent – don't mention birthdays on Monday and Tuesday and forget on Wednesday and Thursday, as some children will miss out and feel hurt by this.

Interview (5 minutes)

Invite one of the leaders (or one of the children) to come and tell the group what Jesus has done for them; how he has helped them in work or school; how he cares for them; how they first made their decision to become a Christian. If the person is very nervous, interview them. If they are more confident, allow them to speak freely, taking notice of the timing allowed for this section.

Worship (10 minutes)

This is a quieter time of worship where songs such as Ishmael's "Father God" can be introduced. Encourage the children who know the words to close their eyes and begin to think about King Jesus. Take your time here; it is important to introduce them to worship.

We instruct the children that praise is generally loud and lively, a time where we have fun singing to God. Worship is where we come closer to God, and think about God more. Worship comes from our hearts and our minds. It involves all our emotions. The definitions of praise and worship may be much broader and more theological than this, but a bite-sized theological portion is more easily swallowed by an eight-year-old.

Preaching Time

The rest of the programme falls under the heading "preaching time". This will include all Bible lessons, illustrations and the story. Take three minutes to explain the rules.

Time for a very special announcement
Inform the children that they are now moving into preaching time, which is the most important thing that happens. Inform them that this section can change their lives. There are special rules: when the whistle blows next, preaching time has begun. In preaching time:

- Nobody leaves to go to the toilet. In fact, nobody moves.
- Anyone talking loses six points straightaway, without discussion.

However, a leader will be walking around with tuck-shop tokens or sweets and will place them in the hands of anyone who really deserves one:

- You must be excellent to receive one. Being good is not enough; anyone can be good.
- You must keep facing the front. If you look at the leader (whom we refer to as a "quiet seat" watcher) he or she will not give you a token/sweet.
- If you get a sweet/token and play with it (or try to open it), it will be taken from you.

Blow the whistle (the whistle can be put away now; it will no longer be needed).

Bible lesson (5 minutes)

There are various ideas to help with the presentation of the Bible lesson:

- Dress some of the children up as characters in the story.
- Use videos. The list of recommended resources in Appendix 4 will give you some ideas.
- If you are presenting the story in narrative form, then tell the story as Hollywood would – don't just read the account.

Illustrations 1–3 (5 minutes each)

Illustrations can take many forms – object lessons, short drama sketches, video clips, testimonies, etc. – basically anything which can be used to present the overall lesson.

Story (10 minutes)

The story is a modern parable which rolls all the themes presented so far into one neat narrative package. Again, various methods can be used to enhance the presentation:

- Use some of the children as characters in the story.
- Draw some of the characters to use as flash cards or acetates.
- Keep it dramatic. Use your body and voice to maximise the presentation.

Prayer/Response (5 minutes)

Always ask for a response. Make an appeal. Ask the children who felt the lesson had applied to them to stand. If the lesson required forgiveness, pray a prayer of forgiveness together. Let the children respond by repeating the prayer after you. There must be a response.

Tomorrow (3 minutes)

Highlight the next day's programme. Keep it exciting: "Tomorrow we'll hear the concluding part of this exciting story," etc.

PROGRAMME ENHANCEMENTS

The role of music within the programme

For the first section until preaching time, music is present almost all the time. Play quiet, ambient music for explaining rules; use loud music for games.
The contrast of total silence in preaching time seems to help the children listen and focus on the discussion.

Preaching

The material you have in front of you is designed to be preached. Preach it with fire and passion, and with gentleness and compassion. Such a proclamation will sometimes bypass the head and speak directly into the heart. The need of the day is children's workers who are full of the Holy Ghost, who will proclaim, in a relevant and contemporary manner, the message of the cross and the principles of God's word.

Don't just tell cute stories – change lives!

This is the part that can't be taught. The message either burns within you or it doesn't. If it burns inside, then lives will be changed. If it doesn't, pray until it does.

Pictures

Many of the illustrations need pictures.
The Internet is a great place to find any piece of artwork you may need. Either use Microsoft Word – go to Insert and then ClipArt and then choose the Internet option; or go to www.ask.com and type in a description of the picture. Another useful source is the computer programme Microsoft Encarta. It is relatively cheap and is a gold mine of pictures on a huge range of topics. In all honesty, the process of getting pictures is more difficult if you don't have access to a computer, but your local library should be a useful place to look. A conversation with the librarian on copyright might be advisable before you start photocopying pictures from books.

Personal references

From time to time the illustrations are from my own personal experiences. In this context I usually use first person narrative. There are two options: probably the best route would be to replace the illustration with one from your own experience. Failing that, tell the story and use the third person: "The person who wrote this book once went to…" or "I know a person who once went to…"

Kim's Quest
Restoring The Treasure

A Series in Five Parts

Introduction

Lesson	Title	Themes covered
1 Topaz	Everyone Has A Purpose	Destiny
2 Emerald	Sort It Out	Forgiving others
3 Amethyst	No Room For Baggage	Letting go of past hurts
4 Ruby	It Gets Tough Sometimes	It isn't always easy being a Christian
5 Sapphire	The Treasure Of Greatest Worth	God's greatest treasure is you

Series Overview

Over the next five days, we will be looking at the life of Jeremiah and working through the story of three friends and their adventure. Each part of the story will involve a precious stone.

The adventure will see the friends recognising their importance and ultimately their value. As the three friends come to understand their self-worth and how valuable they really are, it is my prayer that the children who hear this lesson will also come to understand what it means to be loved and given a destiny by the Creator of the universe.

Construct a table as follows:

Topaz
Emerald
Amethyst
Ruby
Sapphire

It is not a coincidence that the first letters of these words spell "tears" when read downwards. The first letter of each word must be deliberately large to emphasise this.

Also, on one of your side walls you will need to display this poem (after Lesson 1 is finished):

Find the treasure of greatest worth,
This will ensure the future of the earth.
If you succeed then a better place
This world will be for the human race.

Only two friends you may choose,
More than this and you will lose.
If on this quest you should fail,
A sad ending will come to this tale.

1 TOPAZ
Everyone Has A Purpose

	Programme	Item
Section 1	Welcome	
	Rules	
	Prayer	
	Praise	
	Game 1	Island Hopping
	Praise (x2)	
	Fun Item 1	
	Game 2	Treasure Hunters
	Fun Item 2	
	Bible Text	Jeremiah 29:11
	Announcements	
	Interview	
	Worship (x2)	
Section 2	Bible Lesson	Jeremiah (1)
Preaching	Illustration 1	Spectacles
Time	Illustration 2	Drinking Glasses
	Illustration 3	People
	Story	Kim's Quest (1)
	Prayer	

Overview We all have a purpose and a destiny. Not everyone knows that. Jeremiah was chosen before he was born, but there was still some preparation to be done. We too need God to prepare us for the great purpose he has for our lives.

games

Game 1

Island Hopping

PREPARATION Four pieces of cardboard (cut out to look like islands) per team.

PLAYERS Six players per team.

SET-UP Players line up in relay formation at A, with the front member of the team holding the pieces of cardboard.

OBJECT The whole team together must journey from A to B and back, without stepping on anything other than the islands.

WINNING The first team to complete the relay and sit down wins.

Game 2

Treasure Hunters

PREPARATION A black bag full of rubbish and containing five yellow stones* per team is placed at B.

PLAYERS Five per team.

SET-UP Five players line up in relay formation at point A.

OBJECT The first person runs from A to B, searches for a yellow stone and returns to A with it. On returning to A, they tag the next player, who

then repeats the process.

WINNING The first team back and sitting down wins.

* The precious stones that we are using each day will help us to remember the lesson. They can be obtained from most craft shops. You don't need actual topaz, rubies, sapphires, etc. Any stones of matching colour will do.

PreachingTime

BIBLE LESSON ## JEREMIAH (1)

"I will bless you with a future filled with hope – a future of success." (Jeremiah 29:11)

For the next five weeks we will be talking about a man called Jeremiah. He had a few adventures that were very interesting and sometimes very unpleasant.

He was born in a place called Anathoth in Israel. Anathoth was a tiny village in the middle of nowhere. Jeremiah's parents had never done anything really special. He grew up in a place which wasn't particularly special. But Jeremiah was very special. God said to Jeremiah: "Jeremiah, I am your Creator, and before you were born, I chose you to speak for me to the nations."

I think that is absolutely amazing. Before Jeremiah was

even born God had a special job for him to do – a special job which only Jeremiah could do. He was to speak for God. We have a special word for people who speak for God; the word we use is "prophet". A prophet is someone who hears what God is saying and tells others. Jeremiah was a prophet. Even before he was born God had chosen him to be a prophet.

Amazing though it may seem, God also has a special job for us to do. He's chosen us to do something very special for him as well. Some of you may be prophets like Jeremiah; some of you may go to other countries and tell people about Jesus; for others, God may want you to become school teachers, doctors or car mechanics.

We must find out what God wants us to be and do. God has something he wants each and every one of us to do for him.

Spectacles

Object needed: *A pair of spectacles.*

Spectacles are very important to some people. Without them they wouldn't be able to see and they would keep walking into walls and lamp-posts.

Every pair of spectacles is made for a specific purpose. Some people use spectacles to read with – these reading spectacles are made in a special way. Some people use their spectacles to see things that are far away – these people need spectacles that are made for that purpose. Others use their spectacles to see things close up – these people need a different type of spectacles. It depends what the people need. In the same way that every pair of spectacles is different, every person is different. But every person also has a special purpose, something God wants them to do.

Drinking Glasses

Object needed: *A drinking glass and an egg cup (both containing juice).*

A person comes running onto the stage looking and sounding very tired out. They take hold of the egg cup and try to drink the juice.

Egg cups are not very good for drinking juice out

of, are they? One sip and they're empty. It hardly quenches your thirst. It's probably because egg cups are for holding eggs and not for drinking juice out of.

The person then takes the glass and drinks some juice.

That's much better! Glasses are designed for drinking out of. That's their purpose. Everything has a purpose. Spectacles, glasses, even people.

We have a purpose, something God wants us to do.

People

Object needed: *The drinking glass with juice from the previous illustration.*

A person walks onto the stage and tries to drink the juice from the glass used in the previous illustration – except that they try to lift the glass with their nose, then their ear, then their foot…

I can't do this. I want to drink some juice and I can't get it to my mouth. What is the problem? I've tried my nose, my ear, my foot! Why can't I get it to my mouth?

Wait until someone says, "You need to use your hand." Then lift it to your ear and pour!

What's going wrong? I'm using my hand like you said, but it's all running down my neck!

Wait until someone says, "It goes into your mouth."

That's amazing! I can actually drink it very well if I lift it with my hand and drink it with my mouth. I guess the job of my hands is to lift things, and the job of my mouth is to drink things – and my ear? Well, that's probably for hearing things.

When my nose tries to do my hand's job, or my ear tries to do my mouth's job, what a mess!

Every person who is a Christian has been given a special job that God wants them to do. It's important that we try and find out what that job is, or we'll try and do someone else's job and make a mess of it.

Let's find out what God wants us to do, and do it.

● STORY – Kim's Quest (1)

Asil is pronounced "a-seal".

Kim's life had never been very exciting. She had read long stories of the intrepid men who had made their way through the freezing cold and eventually reached the North Pole. She had read with jealousy the stories of the people who were the first to climb Mount Everest, and with even more jealousy of those who later canoed down that mighty mountain. She longed to be like one of the missionaries she heard of in church, who made their way through dense dark jungles in search of people to tell about Jesus. In short, she longed for an adventure.

Kim's life was far from an adventure. Her parents had divorced several years ago. She lived with her mum. She was ten years old. This morning, a Saturday, she had woken up looking for something to do. But, since she had fallen out with her friend Melanie, she had no one to go and play with. Jamie from next door came around to play sometimes, but Kim knew that he had been sleeping at his friend's house and hadn't come back yet. If only Melanie hadn't been so mean to her yesterday and taken her pen without asking. But she had, so Kim definitely wasn't talking to her.

"My life really is very uninteresting," Kim moaned to her mum.

"Cheer up, honey!" her mum replied. "I've got a special job for you to do this afternoon. I want you to go up into the attic and sort out all the old rubbish up there."

"But Mum!" Kim protested. "That's not an adventure. That's a nightmare."

But sure enough, that afternoon Kim found herself up in the dusty old attic trying to sort out what seemed like a million different things. She stacked all the board games. She pushed the old furniture to the side. She collected her old dolls and put them into cardboard boxes. Finally, she took hold of the old wooden chest and began to pull it across to the rest of the furniture. It was very heavy!

"What could possibly be in here?" Kim wondered.

She undid the lock and lifted the lid. There inside was an old painting. It looked like a picture of an island – a desert island. And there in the middle of the island stood an angel. She rubbed some of the dust off the picture and stared at it. For a split second she was sure she could hear the waves; she was sure she could hear the angel speaking; she was sure she heard him say, "So, young Kim. It's an adventure you're looking for, is it?"

Kim just stared at the picture. "I must be imagining things," she thought to herself.

She looked at the picture once again – she was sure the angel's wings were moving. The angel actually looked as if he was getting closer... And then, the angel was there, in the attic! An incredible brightness shone into every corner – Kim could hardly look at him.

"My name is Asil," came the booming voice of the angel.

"You wanted an adventure, Kim. Well, I have one for you. I have a quest for you to fulfil. A quest from the Creator. Do you accept the quest?"

Kim thought very quickly. She was almost too afraid to answer. But she also felt very excited. After all, it wasn't every day that an angel came to visit.

"Will it be dangerous?"

"Oh yes!" Asil replied.

Kim didn't know what to do. But eventually she said, "I accept the quest!"

With that, Asil was gone and all that was left where he had stood was a scroll. A rolled-up scroll. Kim picked it up, opened it and began to read:

> Find the treasure of greatest
> worth,
> This will ensure the future of
> the earth.
> If you succeed then a better
> place
> This world will be for the
> human race.
>
> Only two friends you may
> choose,
> More than this and you will
> lose.
> If on this quest you should
> fail,
> A sad ending will come to this
> tale.

Then, just when she was sure it was a dream, the voice came once more: "Kim, you have four days to complete your quest. Sleep well tonight. You may not sleep so well after that."

Kim finished clearing up the attic at record speed. After she had finished she went to the bathroom and cleaned herself up. But her mind was working overtime. She went to her room and read the scroll again. She placed it on her dressing table next to her favourite stone. Kim had a piece of topaz – a yellow stone that she liked to play with sometimes. She picked it up and held it in her hand.

"You never know," she thought. "This may just be the treasure of greatest worth."

Then she went to bed. She thought about her quest. Now she had a purpose. She was on an adventure.

God has a quest for all of us – a purpose which God has chosen us for. Probably we won't be told what it is by an angel, but that doesn't mean that God doesn't want to speak to us. Maybe right here, right now, God will whisper to us and tell us that he wants us to tell our friends about him. Maybe he'll whisper to us and tell us that one day we'll be missionaries in other nations, telling people about Jesus. We need to begin to listen to God.

Kim closed her eyes. "What will be the treasure of greatest worth?" she thought to herself. "And will I really be able to find it in just four days?"

(To be continued...)

EMERALD
Sort It Out

	Programme	Item
Section 1	Welcome	
	Rules	
	Prayer	
	Praise	
	Game 1	Treasure Chest
	Praise (x2)	
	Fun Item 1	
	Game 2	Restoring The Treasure
	Fun Item 2	
	Bible Text	Matthew 18:35
	Announcements	
	Interview	
	Worship (x2)	
Section 2	Bible Lesson	Jeremiah (2)
Preaching	Illustration 1	Dirty Spectacles
Time	Illustration 2	Dirty Drinking Glasses
	Illustration 3	People
	Story	Kim's Quest (2)
	Prayer	

verview We have all been given a unique and special purpose by God, but before we can fulfil that purpose, we must "get ready". There is a work of preparation that must be done before God can use anyone – this starts with making sure our relationship with God is right, and also our relationship with others.

games Game 2

Game 1

Treasure Chest

PREPARATION A cardboard box per team.

PLAYERS Two players.

SET-UP Players sit at A with their "treasure chest" (the box).

OBJECT The leader calls out all sorts of items that the two people must gather and place in their box. The first team back each time wins a point. Items should include shoes, socks, combs, jumpers, hair bands, etc.

WINNING The team with the most points after ten or so rounds wins.

Make sure that a leader in each team has an emerald*, and then call this out as one of the items to go into the box. Don't give the items back yet. That will form the basis of game 2.

---

* The precious stones that we are using each day will help us to remember the lesson. They can be obtained from most craft shops. You don't need actual topaz, rubies, sapphires, etc. Any stones of matching colour will do.

Restoring The Treasure

PREPARATION The cardboard "treasure chest" from game 1.

PLAYERS Five per team.

SET-UP Five players in relay formation at point A.

OBJECT The first person collects an item from the box and runs from A to B. On their way back to A they must return the treasure to its rightful place. On returning to A, they tag the next player, who then repeats the process.

WINNING The first team to "restore the treasure" wins.

 Preaching Time

BIBLE LESSON JEREMIAH (2)

"If we cannot forgive those who sin against us, God will not forgive us." (Matthew 18:35, paraphrased)

Jeremiah was an amazing man. He had been chosen by God even before he was born. But before he began to serve God,

God said something to him. God said: "Jeremiah, get ready!"

Even though God had chosen Jeremiah before he was born, Jeremiah still had to "get ready". As I said to you last time, God has chosen us as well. He has a special job that only we can do. But God is also saying to us: "Get ready!"

There are some things which we have to do *before* God can let us serve him properly.

Dirty Spectacles

Object needed: *A dirty pair of spectacles.*

We are going to look at the three objects we looked at in Lesson One once again. First, the spectacles.

We said that spectacles are very important to some people. Without them they wouldn't be able to see and they would keep walking into walls and lamp-posts.

But sometimes, even when the spectacles are prepared for a particular need, even though they are the right spectacles for the right person, they're not very good, because they're not clean. They may have bits of dirt on the front. Maybe they've got covered in dust.

Before these spectacles can be of any use, something has to happen to them. Can you guess what? *(You're looking for the answer: "They must be cleaned".)* Likewise, before God uses us, we too need to be clean. The Bible says: "All of us have sinned and fallen short of God's glory."

Dirty Drinking Glasses

Objects needed: *A drinking glass that is obviously dirty; a carton of juice; a bowl containing water and washing-up liquid.*

A person comes running onto the stage looking and sounding very tired out. He or she begins to pour some juice into the glass then, seeing the state of the glass, stops.

Glasses are designed for drinking out of. That's their purpose. Everything has a purpose – spectacles, glasses, even people. But I'm not drinking out of this glass. It's too dirty for me. I'll have to clean it before I can have any juice.

As the person washes the glass, he or she continues to speak.

We have a purpose, something God wants us to do. But God can't use us while there are things wrong in our lives. He can't use us while we are dirty, while we still have sin. Sin is the junk, garbage and rubbish in our lives. While that is still there, God can't use us. But the Bible says, "If we confess our sins to God, he can always be trusted to forgive us and take our sins away."

Illustration 3

People

God really does want to use us. But we have to get ready. We have to make sure that there is nothing between us and God. We must make sure that we have asked God to forgive all the wrong things we've done. But also, before God can use us, we must make sure there is not a problem between us and other people. The Bible says, "If we cannot forgive those who sin against us, God can't forgive us."

So, if you've got a quarrel with a friend, or someone you know, God can't use you until you sort it out. God wants us to do amazing things for him. He has a great purpose for us, but we must make sure that everything is right between us and God, and also between us and other people.

When these things are sorted out, there is nothing God can't do through us.

● Kim's Quest (2)

Kim closed her eyes. "What will be the treasure of greatest worth?" she thought to herself. "And will I really be able to find it in just four days?" It took her quite a while to drop off to sleep, and even when she did she had the strangest feeling she was moving.

Kim woke early in the morning with the sun shining through her curtains. But something was not right. She was sure that she still had that strange rocking feeling that she had felt last night. And another thing: she was fairly sure that these curtains didn't look like her own curtains, and this room looked nothing like her bedroom! Where was she?

She got out of bed and walked across the wooden floor to the window. She pulled back the curtains and couldn't believe what she was seeing. Yesterday morning she'd pulled back her curtains and there was her street and the old familiar trees and the lamp-posts and the boys from across the road playing on their bikes. Today she could see nothing but water – water stretching for kilometres and kilometres.

Kim walked over to the door and opened it. Yesterday there had been a set of stairs going down to the hallway. Today there was instead a set of wooden steps going up. She climbed up the stairs and opened another door. She stepped out and the wind and the spray from the water hit her in the face.

She looked around. She was on a ship, a very old sailing ship! The sails were flapping in the wind. The sun was beating down. The waves were splashing against the sides, and the ship was moving forward at quite a pace.

She read once again the scroll in her hand:

> **Find the treasure of greatest worth,**
> **This will ensure the future of the earth.**
> **If you succeed then a better place**
> **This world will be for the human race.**
>
> **Only two friends you may choose,**
> **More than this and you will lose.**
> **If on this quest you should fail,**
> **A sad ending will come to this tale.**

Then Kim sat down to try and let her mind work out what was going on! "What now?" she thought. "What do I do now?"

She began to shout as loud as she could: "Asil! Where are you? I need some help here!" Suddenly, the wind became calm! The sails stopped moving and a huge angel began to materialise in front of her.

"Hello, Kim! I hope you're making yourself comfortable," said Asil when he had fully appeared. This time he didn't look so bright. He looked like an ordinary person, except, of course, he was seven feet tall.

"Where am I?" Kim demanded. "And what have you done with my bedroom?"

Asil smiled. "Nothing, Kim. You're on your quest, remember? You're heading for that island there."

Kim could just about make out the island in the distance. "But what do I do there?" she asked.

"Oh! It's quite straightforward really! You solve the problems and collect the treasures. If you solve all the problems you will have all the treasures. Then, you must tell me which is the treasure of greatest worth."

Kim thought it all sounded straightforward enough.

"But be warned. If you fail, then your world will suffer. And Kim, I must warn you that I can't always come when you call. I'm one of God's warrior angels. I have other jobs to do as well as looking after little girls on quests. One more thing! Read the second part of the scroll again. You can't do this alone!"

And with that, Asil had

disappeared. The wind had returned and the ship was moving again. Kim looked at the second part of the scroll:

Only two friends you may choose,
More than this and you will lose.

"But who will I choose?" she wondered. She began to think.

"I know I should choose Melanie," she thought. "But she really has been nasty to me. She took my pen without asking."

She thought some more and then decided. She shouted: "I want Jamie to help me!"

For a moment nothing seemed to happen, and then a voice came from behind: "Kim! Where am I?"

Kim turned around to see a rather confused-looking Jamie. Rather calmly, Kim said, "Hello, Jamie! You've come to help me make the world better."

Then, after spending a couple of minutes telling Jamie what was going on, and all the time seeing the island coming closer, and after answering what seemed like 3 million of Jamie's questions, most of which involved warrior angels, Kim was ready to choose her next helper.

"You have to choose Mel," Jamie stated. "You know she'll be excellent at this. She's very clever and she's supposed to be your best friend."

"Well, best friends don't steal each other's pens," Kim replied. And all the time, the island was getting closer. She knew she had to decide before they arrived. Finally Kim gave in. She raised her voice and declared: "I want Mel!"

With that, Melanie appeared, looking even more confused than Jamie – if that was possible. But before asking where she was, Mel looked straight at Kim and said, "I didn't steal your pen. I just borrowed it."

Kim shouted back, "No, you did not!"

Mel shouted, "Yes, I did!"

And if Jamie hadn't jumped in quickly they probably would have ended up hitting each other. Jamie stood between them and said, "Mel! Kim! Stop shouting at each other. We've got a quest to sort out."

Then for the first time Mel looked around. "Where am I?" she began.

Kim looked a bit embarrassed and said, "I've called you here to help me with my quest to make the world a better place."

Mel smiled and then said, "You chose me? So you are still my friend." And with that, and after a lot of explaining, Kim and Melanie hugged and they were the best of friends again.

"Come on, then," Kim shouted. "We'd better get to this island. We have some treasure to find."

But Melanie opened her hand and said, "Maybe this will help." In her hand was an enormous green emerald. Also out of her pocket she pulled a map – a treasure map. *(Place the word Emerald under the word Topaz.)* Then Kim realised. If she hadn't chosen Mel, she never would have got the second treasure.

And we too will never be able to do what God wants us to do unless we have asked God to forgive the wrong things we've done to him and also asked other people to forgive the wrong we've done to them. Maybe we can take a few minutes to pray about those things now.

Finally the ship came close to land and Kim, Jamie and Melanie were able to walk onto the sandy shores. The sun had gone down, the moon was rising and it was time to sleep. That night the three friends slept on the beach, not knowing that someone was watching them. They had three days left to complete their search for the treasure of greatest worth.

(To be continued…)

3 AMETHYST
No Room For Baggage

	Programme	Item
Section 1	Welcome	
	Rules	
	Prayer	
	Praise	
	Game 1	Treasure Makers
	Praise (x2)	
	Fun Item 1	
	Game 2	Treasure Seekers
	Fun Item 2	
	Bible Text	1 Peter 5:7
	Announcements	
	Interview	
	Worship (x2)	
Section 2 Preaching Time	Bible Lesson	Jeremiah (3)
	Illustration 1	Carrying Alone
	Illustration 2	What's In The Bag?
	Illustration 3	Running The Race
	Story	Kim's Quest (3)
	Prayer	

Overview To complete God's quest we need to learn to travel light. We must drop all the baggage of unforgiveness, hurt, bitterness and resentment and run the race God has mapped out for us with diligence.

Game 1

Treasure Makers

PREPARATION   Cut out the individual letters of the word AMETHYST for each team and place them at B.

PLAYERS   Four per team.

SET-UP   Players go to point A.

OBJECT   The players run from A in relay formation, collect a letter at B and return to A. This repeats until all the letters are back.

WINNING   The first team to construct the word AMETHYST and sit down wins.

On completion, show the children an amethyst.

Game 2

Treasure Seekers

PREPARATION   While the children watch (but the players don't), several purple stones* are hidden in the room.

PLAYERS   Three from each team.

---

* The precious stones that we are using each day will help us to remember the lesson. They can be obtained from most craft shops. You don't need actual topaz, rubies, sapphires, etc. Any stones of matching colour will do.

SET-UP   Three players in relay formation stand at point A.

OBJECT   The first person runs from A, finds a purple stone (helped by a shouting team) and returns to point B.

WINNING   The team to collect five amethysts first wins.

PreachingTime

BIBLE LESSON   **JEREMIAH (3)**

"God cares for you, so turn all your worries over to him." (1 Peter 5:7)

Jeremiah didn't have an easy job. What God had told him to say to the people was not the nicest message to have to bring.

Jeremiah had to tell the people that because they had done wrong things (things the Bible calls sin), God was going to punish them by allowing a foreign army to come and to take them all away as prisoners.

God didn't do this because the people had sinned. He did this because, even though he'd told the people again and again to live right and to do right things, they'd kept ignoring God's warnings. And so, even though God loves people very much, he can't allow sin to carry on forever.

The people didn't like to hear what Jeremiah had to say. They didn't want to be told that they would be taken away and become slaves in a different land. They hated Jeremiah. Many of them were very cruel to him. But Jeremiah kept speaking the message God had told him to. He was very brave indeed. Even though the people kept saying bad things to Jeremiah and they were cruel to him, Jeremiah kept telling them what God wanted them to hear. He didn't keep the hurts and pains in his heart. He kept giving them to God.

Jeremiah knew that he would end up with lots of hurts, but he knew that he would always be wise to give all his hurts to God.

It isn't wrong to get hurt. Everyone gets hurt at some point in their lives. But we should never keep those hurts, or hold on to them; they will stop us completing our quest. We must give our hurts to God.

Person 1: *(Dragging the bag)* This is so heavy.
Person 2: That looks heavy.
Person 1: *(Still dragging)* It *is* very heavy.
Person 2: How far do you have to go?
Person 1: To the other side of the stage.
Person 2: That far? That's quite a long way. Do you want some help?
Person 1: *(Still dragging)* Oh no! I like to carry my own baggage, thank you.
Person 2: Why?
Person 1: I think it is good for me to carry this bag myself.
Person 2: Why?
Person 1: Stop asking me these silly questions.

Eventually Person 1 falls down and shouts.

Person 1: OK! Help me then.
Person 2: *(Dragging together now)* See, it's easier with two.

The two people remain for the next illustration.

Illustration 1

Carrying Alone

Object needed: *A sports bag.*

You will need either to load the bag with heavy objects, or pretend it is heavy.

Illustration 2

What's In The Bag?

Object needed: *The words "hurts", "revenge" and "unforgiveness" must be in the bag, written on flash paper*.*

Person 3: What are you two doing?

Person 1+2: We're carrying this bag.

Person 1: It's easier with two.

Person 3: Are you sure you should be carrying it?

Person 1: Of course! It's my bag.

Person 3: But what's in it?

Person 1: Just things.

Person 3: What things?

Person 1: Oh, just things!

Person 3: Show me.

Person 1 opens the bag and takes out the first piece of paper.

Person 3: It says "unforgiveness".

Person 1: Yes! I got it when Ashley broke my bike and I promised I'd never forgive him.

Person 2: I didn't know you had that stuff in there. This is nothing to do with me – I'm out of here.

Person 2 walks off. Person 1 takes out the next item.

Person 3: It says "hurts".

Person 1: Yes! I got it when Tina next door was really horrible to me.

Person 3: When was that?

Person 1: Oh, about five years ago.

Person 1 takes out the final item.

Person 3: It says "revenge".

Person 1: Yes! Mr Harold across the road burst my ball when it went over his fence for the fiftieth time last year. So when I'm a bit bigger I'm going to smash all his windows.

Person 3: But that's terrible!

Person 1: I know! That ball cost me £1.99.

Person 3: No, not that! You, wanting to smash his windows. In fact, you shouldn't be carrying any of these things. You're supposed to give them all to God. You have to forgive people and let things go. You have

to give all your
hurts to God.

Person 1: I know! But it's
really hard to let go.

Person 3: But you have to. Let
me show you why!

* Flash paper is available from
www.tricksfortruth.com

Running The Race

Object needed: *A runner,
person 1, taking
up his position,
looking as if
he's about to
start a race.*

Person 3: Look, he's ready to
start his race. On
your marks, get set,
go!

*The runner begins to run
frantically – on the spot of course.
Person 3 commentates.*

Person 3: *(In commentator voice)*
And our runner is off
to an amazing start,
leaving everyone else
miles behind. He is
clearly the fastest and
the best. No one can
catch him; surely he
will win…

(To Person 2) But
watch this.

*Person 3 picks up the bag and
hands it to the runner.*

Person 3: Just hold this for me
please, mate!

*The runner takes the bag and
collapses under its weight.*

Person 3: *(In commentator voice
again)* Oh dear. It's all
gone terribly wrong.
Everyone is
overtaking him. He'll
never finish the race
now.

The runner remains on the ground.

Person 3: You see! With all
those bad things, he
could never finish
the race. We too have
a race to run – not an
actual race, more
something we have
to do in our lives for
God. But if we keep
holding on to all
these bad things,
we'll never do
anything for God.

Person 1: So how do I get rid of
all this stuff?

Person 3: You pray and ask God
to take it away.

Person 1: *(Praying)* God, there's
a lot of bad things
here. Will you take
them away, please? I
forgive Ashley for
breaking my bike.

Person 3 sets fire to flash paper with the word "unforgiveness".

Person 1: And I forgive Tina for being horrible to me.

Person 3 sets fire to flash paper with the word "hurts".

Person 1: *(Stops praying)* Do I have to forgive Mr Harold too?!
Person 3: Yes!
Person 1: Oh well! *(Prays)* And I forgive Mr Harold and I won't smash his windows.

Person 3 sets fire to flash paper with the word "revenge".

Person 3: Feels better, doesn't it?
Person 1: Yes, I guess it does.

● Kim's Quest (3)

Finally the ship came close to land and Kim, Jamie and Mel were able to walk onto the sandy shores. The sun had gone down, the moon was rising and it was time to sleep. That night the three friends slept on the beach, not knowing that someone was watching them. They had three days left to complete their search for the treasure of greatest worth.

The three friends awoke early the next morning. The sky above them was blue; the sun was shining brightly. But Kim, Melanie and Jamie weren't in the sun at all. They were surrounded by a large group of people. The friends couldn't see clearly the faces of those that surrounded them, because they were silhouetted by the sun. But they were clearly very tall and extremely thin. For some time they just stood and stared at the three friends. Then the tallest person spoke. It was a deep resonating voice. It said: "You are carrying a lot of baggage. You will never finish your quest with all that!"

Kim was surprised. She looked at her friends. None of them had any baggage, not even a carrier bag. She knew she wasn't carrying anything, so she was naturally confused.

The person looked again for some time and then said, "Your hearts are carrying a lot of baggage. And now you will see what you are carrying."

The person mumbled some words, and then all the people were gone. Everything seemed as it was before. The sky was very blue; the sun shone brightly; the sea lightly broke onto the sand. Jamie was the first to speak: "Well! I have no idea what that was about, but if we're going to complete this quest in the next three days we had better get on with it."

The three friends got to their feet and looked at the map. It had an "x" marking a place called "greatest treasure". They set off towards a path which led them into the trees. But as they walked they suddenly felt something on their backs. All three friends were now carrying rucksacks, and, try as they might, they couldn't shift them. They seemed almost glued on. They felt quite heavy, but certainly not too heavy to walk with.

They made their way into the woods and up a path that led gently up the side of a hill. The trees crowded in on both sides, but there was plenty of room to walk. The sun was blazing, the sky was blue and a gentle breeze blew in from the sea. Jamie, who was at the back, shouted, "It's very nice, this quest, isn't it?"

"More like a holiday in Spain," Melanie responded. But Kim said nothing. She was sure that there would be more to it than this, and she didn't want to become too comfortable.

When they had started out, the rucksacks they carried seemed bearable. Now the sun was beginning to set, the top of the hill still looked some distance away and the rucksacks were starting to feel heavy. As they walked, Jamie was sure he heard a loud crashing sound in the trees. Then they all heard it: "Bang! Crash! Stamp!"

Kim walked over to the edge of the trees and stared in. Then she screamed.

"Run! It's a rhinoceros! It's coming this way!"

The three friends rushed further into the woods as fast as they could. The rhinoceros must have picked up their scent and changed course to charge after them. They ran through some branches that scratched their faces, through brambles that ripped their clothes and through mud that soaked their feet. But all that was better than a rhinoceros hitting you with his huge horn. They ran and ran deeper into the woods with the animal getting closer and closer. He was only a half-metre away from Melanie when Kim shouted, "Jump!" The three friends jumped sideways into what they thought was a pile of mud. The rhinoceros was too big and too heavy to stop. It kept on running into the distance.

"Phew! That was a close one," shouted Jamie.

"I thought we were going to get squashed," responded Kim.

"I don't think we're in the clear yet!" came Melanie's shaking voice. As Jamie and Kim looked round they could see that Melanie was up to her waist in the mud and sinking fast. But before they had a chance to help her, they too began to sink. Before long they were up to their chests in mud. Kim began shouting frantically: "Asil! Asil! Where are you? Help us!"

Kim prayed: "God, we desperately need your help! Send Asil, your angel, to help us." Nothing happened, but Kim was sure she heard a voice in her head whispering: "This time you must help yourself, Kim."

She looked at her friends. They were all up to their necks now. "Get the rucksacks off!" she hollered. But, try as they might, the rucksacks wouldn't come off their backs.

"I've got it!" shouted Jamie. "The rucksacks won't come off because they are a part of us. The strange people took the things which were in our hearts and put them on our backs. What does mine say?"

Kim stretched round and read the word. "BULLIES! Yours says BULLIES!" she exclaimed.

Jamie's mind flashed back to the playground. He was seven years old and surrounded by a circle of big boys who were four or five years older than him. They were pushing him from one part of the circle to the other and all the time calling him names. They had already taken his dinner money. Then one of them punched him in the nose. He felt the blood beginning to pour. He slumped to his knees crying.

Jamie knew what was going on. He had never forgiven those bullies. He hated what they had done to him, he hated the way that they had humiliated him, and he hated having to miss his lunch. He began to sink lower. "OK! OK!" he shouted. "I forgive them. They did upset me a lot, but I forgive them."

Then an amazing thing happened. Instead of sinking, he started being pushed up, until he was standing on dry ground again. His rucksack had gone. He looked down at Kim and Melanie, and explained quickly:

"All the stuff that's hurt you, and that you haven't forgiven people for, is in your heart. You have to forgive to drop the rucksack, or you will sink. Mel, turn round! Let me see yours."

The word DEATH was written there.

"What does that mean?" asked Jamie. But Melanie knew. She never talked about it with anyone. She hid it deep in her heart. "I used to have a little sister," she sobbed, "but some stupid man knocked her down with his car."

Melanie knew that it hadn't been the driver's fault, but she couldn't forgive him anyway. She had hated the driver. She'd even had dreams of growing up and buying a car just so she could knock him down. But Melanie knew that her hate and her desire for revenge was wrong. She knew she would have to forgive. "I forgive him," she sobbed. "I forgive him."

Sure enough, the rucksack disappeared and she was pushed back to solid ground.

"Now what's on yours?" Jamie asked Kim, who was disappearing fast.

The word DIVORCE was written on Kim's rucksack. "It's your parents' divorce, Kim," Jamie said. "What happened?"

Kim's mind flashed back to the nights of constant shouting in her house – nights when her dad came home late and hollered at her mum; nights when Kim came in from playing and found her mum crying. She hated her dad.

"Kim, you have to forgive him," Jamie and Mel urged. Kim was sinking fast. She had to decide. She didn't like what her dad had done, but she knew what she had to do.

"I forgive him!" she shouted.

And, just like Jamie and Mel before her, she was back on solid ground.

We too may have hurts in our hearts that will weigh us down and stop us completing the quest God has for us. Let's take a couple of minutes to pray and ask God to help us forgive those who've hurt us.

The friends were covered in mud. But they felt much better. Their hearts didn't carry any more of that nasty baggage. They saw a waterfall in the distance and headed towards it to get cleaned up. The gushing water soon swept away the mud. Then Melanie looked across and asked, "Jamie, what have you got in your hair?"

It looked like a ball of mud. But when Mel took it and washed it in the waterfall it glistened brightly, a lovely purple colour. It was an amethyst – the third jewel. *(Place the word Amethyst under the word Emerald.)*

As the sun finally went down and Kim, Melanie and Jamie lay down for the night, they knew that they only had two days to go. And they still didn't know where to find the treasure of greatest worth.

Tomorrow they would arrive at a very special place.

(To be continued…)

RUBY
It Gets Tough Sometimes

	Programme	Item
Section 1	Welcome	
	Rules	
	Prayer	
	Praise	
	Game 1	Treasure Map
	Praise (x2)	
	Fun Item 1	
	Game 2	Fill The Treasure Chest
	Fun Item 2	
	Bible Text	Jeremiah 6:16
	Announcements	
	Interview	
	Worship (x2)	
Section 2	Bible Lesson	Jeremiah (4)
Preaching	Illustration 1	Two Paths
Time	Illustration 2	Testimony
	Illustration 3	Rubies
	Story	Kim's Quest (4)
	Prayer	

**verview** Not everything is easy when you're a Christian. Not everything falls conveniently into place. Sometimes things are difficult; sometimes things are hard. But true Christians keep on going.

games

Game 1

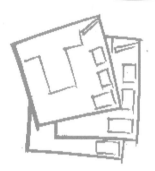

Treasure Map

PREPARATION Make three copies of a map of the room in which you hold your activities. Mark on the map the locations of ten rubies (red stones)* which you have pre-placed. Also copy a fourth map onto acetate and display it on the OHP so that all the children can see the locations of the stones.

PLAYERS Four per team.

SET-UP All players stand at A with a map per team.

OBJECT The teams go out together or split up. They have to collect the rubies (red stones).

WINNING The team with the most rubies (red stones) after two minutes wins.

* The precious stones that we are using each day will help us to remember the lesson. They can be obtained from most craft shops. You don't need actual topaz, rubies, sapphires, etc. Any stones of matching colour will do.

Fill The Treasure Chest

PREPARATION Lots and lots of coloured stones* in a box at A. A box per team at B.

PLAYERS Three from each team.

SET-UP Three players line up in relay formation at point A.

OBJECT The first person runs from A to a point about two metres before B (mark the point with a masking-tape line), carrying a coloured stone. He or she then throws the stone into the box, returns to A and the next person goes.

WINNING The team with the most stones in its box wins.

Preaching Time

BIBLE LESSON JEREMIAH (4)

"When you stood at the crossroads, I [God] told you, 'Follow the road your ancestors took, and you will find peace.'" (Jeremiah 6:16)

Doing the things God wants us to do is not always easy. Jeremiah learned that himself.

He knew that telling people what God wanted them to know wouldn't make him popular.

Doing the things God wants us to do will mean doing things we don't always like doing. Jeremiah told the people of Israel that God was saying to them, "Follow the road your ancestors took and you will find peace."

He was asking them to walk an old path, a path that not many people walked. It would be a difficult path, but if they walked it, they would find peace. He was telling the people of Israel to do what God wanted, and, even though it might seem hard at times, it was the best way.

Jeremiah himself is a good example of a person who serves God and doesn't always find it easy. Just because he told the people what God was saying, he was put in prison, he was thrown down a well and he was mocked by many people. But when God eventually sent in the Assyrian army to take the people of Israel away, God kept Jeremiah safe, just as he had promised.

Walking the way God wants isn't always easy. But God really does protect us and keep us safe.

Illustration 1

Two Paths

Objects needed: *Six cans of Coke.*

You will need a volunteer for this illustration. Choose a "sensible" volunteer who won't give you "silly" answers. Explain this to the volunteers.

Here are two paths. You can't see them, but I will describe them to you.

The first path is a very easy-looking path. It is nice and straight. There are no trees or bushes at the sides, so no one will be able to jump out and attack you. The sun shines nicely on this path. It's the ideal path, with no jagged stones or nasty holes. It's a great path really.

The second path is altogether different. It isn't so straight; it has some quite severe bends. There are lots of brambles at the sides and some of them are growing onto the path. In fact, I'd say it was a path that not many people used. There are places where attackers could hide, and then jump out and attack you. The sun shines on it, but it also rains here, and sometimes there are even hailstones. It's not the nicest path I'd ever want to go for a walk on.

If you had to choose which path you'd like to walk down, which would you choose? *(Wait for a response.)* Of course, you would choose the easier path. Most sensible people would.

But suppose I said to you, "If you walk down that harder path for one mile, you'll get these cans of Coke. And if you walk down that first great path for one mile you'll get nothing at all." Which path would you choose then? *(Wait for a response.)* Fair enough! If you choose the harder path, you get a reward. That seems to be a good reason for walking the harder path.

If you live your life as a Christian, it might be harder – it might not – but at the end of it you are guaranteed to go to heaven and live forever with God. If you don't live your life as a Christian, you don't live forever with God.

Now, suppose I said to you, "If you walk down the harder path, it might be more difficult, but it'll be much more exciting than the nice path. Dangers may come, but God will always look after you. Things may sometimes go wrong, but God will always keep you safe. If you walk down the other path, it might be easier – it might not – but there will be nobody protecting you, nobody keeping you safe. There'll be no

excitement." Which path would you choose?

You see, if you choose to live as a Christian, it won't always be easy, but God will always protect you. It might get tough sometimes, but it'll be very exciting.

Which path will you choose? Will you be a Christian, or not?

Testimony

Invite a capable child or a leader to come and talk about what it means to be a Christian. It is important, in order to flow with the theme, that they point out times when it has been difficult, but that God always looks after them.

Rubies

Object needed: *A ruby or a red stone*

Rubies look very nice, but they also have all sorts of exciting uses. Did you know that rubies are used to focus the beam of a laser? Does anyone know how to make rubies? (Take some responses.)

It's not dissimilar to the way that diamonds are made. Certain chemicals are trapped very, very deep underground. And then the ground pushes them from all directions. They are put under immense pressure. It would squash a person to nothing. But the pressure over many years eventually produces this lovely ruby.

A similar process happens with people. Some of the loveliest people I know have had to cope with some very bad things. For example, some people's parents split up; some never even knew their parents; some were orphans; some are disabled and have had to cope with difficulties. But because of those things they have learned to ask God to help. They have learned to trust God. And they are some of the nicest people I know.

Sometimes, pressure on us makes us much better than we were before. Sometimes God allows bad things to happen to us because he knows it will make us better people.

● Kim's Quest (4)

As the sun finally went down and Kim, Melanie and Jamie lay down for the night, they knew that they only had two days to go. And they still didn't know where to find the treasure of greatest worth.

Kim awoke early the next morning and looked at the map that Asil had given her.

"Come on, everyone!" she said. "Time to get moving! This is our last-but-one day, remember, and if this map is right we have a long way to go today if we are to get to the other side of the island by tomorrow."

Melanie and Jamie woke slowly. Their tummies were informing them that they hadn't eaten properly for some time, and this adventure didn't seem so exciting on an empty stomach. They drank some water from the waterfall. They ate some coconut which Jamie had dragged down from one of the trees. And then they set off.

The sun seemed hotter than ever. The breeze from the sea had disappeared and the three friends felt very tired. It took them several hours to walk up the hill beside the waterfall, and even when they reached the top the path was far from pleasant. Brambles were tangled with nettles and they found that walking was hard work. Jamie, who was normally very positive, began to complain about the long journey. Melanie had a blister on the heel of her foot which was becoming unbearable, and even Kim, who had longed so much for an exciting adventure, was beginning to feel sad.

Eventually they came to a point where the path split in

two. One path moved further up the hill and the other stretched downwards. They could now see the beach beneath them and longed to be on it. They would have loved to go splashing in the cold refreshing sea.

Kim opened the map and the three friends stared at it. It was clear to everyone that the map was pointing them to go up the hill.

"But the path's going to come out on the beach eventually," Jamie protested. "Why should we go up and down a stupid hill just to end up in the same place? Let's just go straight down this path here to the beach now."

Kim was tired as well, but she knew that she should follow the map. They argued for some time, until they decided to take a vote.

"All those in favour of going straight to the beach," Jamie said, "hands up now!" Jamie put his hand up. "All those in favour of going over this stupid hill," he continued, "hands up now!" Kim put her hand up. "Well, that's one vote for each. I guess it's down to you, Mel."

Melanie was really under pressure. She didn't want to hurt Kim's feelings and she didn't want to upset Jamie. She really was finding it difficult to choose. Just then something unusual happened. About 50 metres down the path towards the beach, the strange people appeared again. The tallest of the group, the one who had talked to them before, spoke to the three friends, his deep voice carrying easily through the silence.

"Well done, children! You have earned your reward. Come this way; we have prepared this feast for you." Then the strange people moved aside to reveal a banquet. There were sandwiches and cakes; there was pop, ice cream, trifle and biscuits.

"But Asil told me to follow the path," Kim shouted. The strangers said nothing. Melanie looked at the food. She was so hungry. Her tummy had been rumbling for a long time.

"That's it," she declared. "I'm going down this path."

"Hurrah!" shouted Jamie, and took off after her. Kim just stood and watched. Her friends rushed to the food and began to eat. But, as they bit into the food, it turned to sand. Jamie spat it out quickly. "What's this?" he demanded.

"This is a test – that's what this is!" the tallest stranger responded. And with that, to Kim's horror, a cage suddenly appeared around her two friends. The man went on: "Bring us all the treasures by tomorrow, Kim, or your friends will die."

The people suddenly vanished, along with her friends. Kim stood transfixed. What was she to do now? She couldn't complete this quest on her own. **Sometimes God's way may seem harder, but God will** always look after us if we walk the way he wants us to. If we are determined to do what God wants us to do, he will keep us safe.

"It's time to eat, Kim." It was the soothing voice of Asil.

Kim spun around: "Where are my friends, Asil?"

"They were told to follow the map. The hill may look harder, but it is safer," Asil responded. "Now eat." Asil handed Kim some food. Then he gave her something to drink. Kim felt something gritty in her mouth. She put her fingers in to pull out what was there. As they came out, there in her fingers was a ruby. It was a bright red precious stone. Kim stared at the stone. She would have loved to be feeling excited, but she just felt sad. She had lost her friends. *(Place the word Ruby on the list underneath Amethyst.)*

"Now sleep, Kim," said Asil. "You must still bring me the treasure of greatest worth."

Kim felt her eyelids begin to droop. She was so tired. She was so sad. She was on her own. She began to fall asleep, hoping that somehow tomorrow would be better. How was she to bring the treasures to the strangers *and* bring the treasure of greatest worth to Asil? What was she going to do?

I'll let you know very soon.

(To be continued...)

SAPPHIRE
The Treasure of Greatest Worth

	Programme	Item
Section 1	**Welcome**	
	Rules	
	Prayer	
	Praise	
	Game 1	Treasure Map
	Praise (x2)	
	Fun Item 1	
	Game 2	Fill The Treasure Chest
	Fun Item 2	
	Bible Text	John 11:35
	Announcements	
	Interview	
	Worship (x2)	
Section 2	**Bible Lesson**	Jeremiah (5)
Preaching	**Illustration 1**	Value
Time	**Illustration 2**	My Mum!
	Illustration 3	Mother Teresa
	Story	Kim's Quest (5)
	Prayer	

Overview There is nothing more valuable in all of creation than humankind. God sent his only Son to die for people. Jesus wept over people. The Bible even tells us that God loves us in exactly the same way that he loves Jesus. We are the treasure of greatest worth.

games

We are going to repeat the games from Lesson 4. This time, however, the various kinds of different-coloured stones are hidden and are all worth different points:

> topaz – 5, emeralds – 6, amethysts – 7, rubies – 8, sapphires – 10

Don't tell the children the values of the stones. Simply point out that there is a precious stone which we haven't talked about yet, though it is worth the most points. At the end of the game, award ten bonus points to the team that can guess the name of the stone of greatest worth.

Treasure Map

PREPARATION Make three copies of a map of the room in which you hold your activities. Mark on the map the locations of ten rubies (red stones)* which you have pre-placed. Also copy a fourth map onto acetate and display it on the OHP

---

* The precious stones that we are using each day will help us to remember the lesson. They can be obtained from most craft shops. You don't need actual topaz, rubies, sapphires, etc. Any stones of matching colour will do.

so that all the children can see the locations of the stones.

PLAYERS Four per team.

SET-UP All players stand at A with a map per team.

OBJECT The teams go out together or split up. They have to collect the rubies (red stones).

WINNING The team with the most rubies (red stones) after two minutes wins.

Fill The Treasure Chest

PREPARATION Lots of coloured stones* in a box at A. An empty box per team at B.

PLAYERS Three from each team.

SET-UP Three players line up in relay formation at point A.

OBJECT The first person runs from A to a point about two metres before B – mark the point with a masking-tape line – carrying a coloured stone. He or she then throws the stone into the box, returns to A and the next person goes.

WINNING The team with the stones of most accumulated value wins.

PreachingTime

Illustration 1

BIBLE LESSON JEREMIAH (5)

"Jesus wept."
(John 11:35,
New International
Version)

Jeremiah is often called "the weeping prophet" because he wept openly about the wrong things that the people of Israel did. He would also cry because nobody would listen to him.

Jeremiah did not cry because he was weak. And it wasn't because of a nasty and gloomy personality that he told the people about the bad things that would happen to them if they didn't stop doing bad things. He cried because he loved his people and he loved God.

Jeremiah was very sensitive and wept because the people wouldn't turn back to God. Jeremiah loved the people so much that he wept.

Over 500 years later, another man could be seen crying, and crying for the same reason as Jeremiah. This man was crying because he didn't want to see the people he loved not going to heaven. He was crying because he loved people more than anything else in all of creation.

His name was Jesus. He was the Son of God.

Value

Objects needed: *A video clip of the crucifixion (there are many to choose from), a chocolate bar, a can of pop, a games console.*

The more something is worth, the more you are willing to pay for it.

This is a chocolate bar. It's worth about 30p, so you'd be willing to pay 30p for it.

This is a can of pop. It's worth about 50p, so you'd be willing to pay 50p for it.

This is a computer. It's worth about £150, so you'd be willing to pay £150 for it.

Some things are harder to put prices on. There's a story in the old part of the Bible about a man who worked for fourteen years so that he could marry the woman he loved.

How much do you think a person might be worth? Now Jesus was prepared to do this... *(Show the video clip.)*

The Bible says, "With this blood Jesus purchased people for God." You were worth so much that Jesus was willing to die for you.

Illustration 2

My Mum!

As with all allusions to personal situations, you should replace the story listed with a similar one from your own experience – in this case, your own childhood experiences.

How many of you have ever had chicken pox?

When I was much younger I had this horrible illness called "chicken pox". Some of you may have had chicken pox. It isn't very pleasant, is it?

It was a very bad case – I couldn't go to school for three weeks. Some of you may think that was good. But I hated it. I had nothing to do all day because all my friends were at school, and I couldn't sleep at night because the chicken pox made me itch so much. I was covered in this horrible pink cream – I looked like Mr Blobby – but it didn't stop me itching.

One night it was so bad, I lay in my bed crying. My mum came in to see if I was all right. She saw how upset I was and she said something incredible. She said: "If I could have chicken pox instead of you, I would!"

Now my mum didn't really want chicken pox. Nobody does. But because she loved me

so much she would rather have had chicken pox than see me suffer. She said it just because she loved me.

Jesus loves me too. He loved me so much that he wanted to take a terrible disease away from me – not chicken pox, but sin. He loved me so much that he took all my sin onto himself and died on a cross so that one day I would have the chance to go to heaven.

I must be very special for Jesus to do that for me. He also died on that cross for you. He loves you very much as well.

Illustration 3

Mother Teresa

Object needed: *A picture of Mother Teresa.*

Mother Teresa was born in Albania in 1910. She spent most of her life in India, taking care of poor people. She died in 1997, but in her lifetime she founded many orphanages and took care of the poor.

India is not the easiest place for a missionary to live. Recently, many Christians were murdered there just for telling others about God. During her time in India several wars broke out, and many missionaries fled the country. But Mother Teresa

stayed. She refused to leave. Despite the great dangers, Mother Teresa lived in India, helping the poor and looking after orphans, until she died there in 1997.

Mother Teresa didn't stay in India through all the trouble and problems because she was forced to. She stayed there helping the poor because she loved the people. She knew how much God loved them and she wanted to make sure that she showed that love to the people of India.

● Kim's Quest (5)

Kim felt her eyelids begin to droop. She was so tired. She was so sad. She was on her own. She began to fall asleep, hoping that somehow tomorrow would be better. How was she to bring the treasures to the strangers *and* bring the treasure of greatest worth to Asil? What was she going to do?

The rest of Kim's quest didn't seem exciting at all. She continued her journey to the top of the hill. Ahead of her, lying on what looked like a sundial, was the final precious stone. It was a dark blue stone –

a large sapphire. Kim picked it up and placed it in her pocket. *(Add Sapphire to the list under Ruby.)*

She had them all! Five days had passed since the quest began and now in her hand she held the five precious stones: the yellow topaz, the green emerald, the purple amethyst, the red ruby, and now the blue sapphire. She wondered which one was the "treasure of greatest worth". She remembered the poem:

> Find the treasure of greatest
>   worth,
> This will ensure the future of
>   the earth.
> If you succeed then a better
>   place
> This world will be for the
>   human race.
>
> Only two friends you may
>   choose,
> More than this and you will
>   lose.
> If on this quest you should
>   fail,
> A sad ending will come to
>   this tale.

This should have been an exciting moment. But Kim didn't feel excited at all. The poem made her think of her friends. She was lonely. She wanted to know where her friends had gone.

Kim didn't have to wonder for long. As she approached the edge of the hill, which descended rapidly back down towards the beach, she could see her friends there. They were still in the cage. The strangers were standing perfectly still watching Jamie and Mel in the cage. They made no movement at all; they looked as if they were waiting for something. Then Kim realised at last: they were waiting for her. She made her way down the steep hill, taking care not to fall.

She walked towards the waiting strangers. They looked almost like statues. When Kim was only 50 metres away, they turned and looked at her. Kim walked closer. She could see Melanie and Jamie sitting on the floor of the cage. She approached more slowly now, more cautiously. But the strangers did nothing. They simply waited until Kim was standing right in front of them, and then the leader spoke: "Welcome, Kim. We have been waiting and watching. We saw you collect the final precious stone from the ground. Now you have all five stones."

Kim simply stood and listened. She was very afraid, but she was far more concerned with her friends' safety. The leader continued: "Do you want your friends back, Kim? Do you really want them back?"

"Of course I want them back!" Kim retorted, surprising herself with how much force she put into the reply. "Give my friends back now!"

"By all means!" the leader responded. "But it will cost you. If you want your friends back, you will have to give me the precious stones."

"But," Kim started, "I must take these to Asil. That is my quest. I am to bring Asil the treasure of greatest worth. If I don't, the world will get worse!"

The leader said nothing. He stood and waited. Kim was stuck. She had to give up the treasure or she would never see her friends again. She looked at the five precious stones: topaz, emerald, amethyst, ruby, sapphire. She didn't have to think for long. She walked over to the stranger and placed them in his hand.

"Take them. My friends are worth much more than these stones."

The stranger took the stones and immediately the cage opened. Melanie and Jamie rushed out. They all hugged each other.

"Well," said Kim, "we might as well go back to the ship. There's no way we can find any more treasure, and our time is up." The three friends walked towards the ship, unaware that behind them an angel had appeared and was busily talking to a tall stranger.

"What do you think?" Asil asked the tall stranger.

"I think you have chosen well, Asil. She is a very good choice indeed. Still, she has yet to tell you what the treasure of greatest worth is."

"I think she'll know," Asil replied. With that, the cage and the strangers and Asil disappeared.

Kim and her friends made their way to the ship. Once on board they found some food and drink and sat down to eat. As they sat, Asil appeared before them; he shone brighter than the sun. "Kim, what is the treasure of greatest worth?" His voice seemed to boom louder than the water from the waterfall.

"I don't have it!" Kim said. "The strangers took it."

"Kim! What is the treasure of greatest worth?" Asil repeated.

Kim was shaking. She had lost the stones – surely Asil knew this? Then all at once she knew the answer. What had been more important to her than the precious stones? What had been worth giving up those precious gems for?

"My friends!" Kim shouted. "They are the treasure of greatest worth! And all the boys and girls of the world – they are the treasures of greatest worth. It's not the stones, it's the people. The boys and girls of the world are the treasure of greatest worth!"

Asil stopped glowing. His voice became calm and sombre: "You have answered rightly, Kim. Well done. The precious stones were just a clue. If you take the "t" from topaz, and the "e" from emerald, and the "a" from amethyst, and the "r" from ruby, and the "s" from sapphire, you form the word "tears". And 2,000 years ago my Lord and Master Jesus wept tears of sorrow because he loved you so much, you and the children of the world. Tell them all, Kim – tell them all that Jesus loves them."

Kim just stared. She knew God loved people, but until now she hadn't realised how much.

"Now, Kim! You have done well. You have completed the quest. But this is not the end, Kim. God tests only those he wants to use. King Jesus has many things that he wants you to do, Kim. We will meet again."

With that, Asil was gone. The island also disappeared. The three friends continued eating their meal. But that night as they made their way below deck, they knew that they would wake in their own beds the following morning. The quest was over. Well, at least for now.

Craft
activities

CRAFT BACKGROUND INFORMATION

The craft pages break down into three main sections:

- There is one main craft idea, called "Kim's Island". A small group of possibly older children may undertake this as a project through the week using the day-to-day guide.
- There are also five daily crafts for the main group to follow.
- Finally, there are several "alternative" crafts for those who don't want to do that particular day's activity.

I recommend preparing your craft area with a selection of storage boxes that the children can help themselves to. This is all about choice and freedom of expression. Show the children what they can make, but don't do it for them in a *Blue Peter* step-by-step way. The storage boxes should contain things like paper, pens, paint, bottle tops, toilet roll tubes, tissue paper, card, glue (glue sticks), glitter, scrap materials, and all the items listed on the following pages. Keep each box well stocked. This also enables the children to come to the craft area during free play (see "Daily Format") and make some things that you hadn't scheduled – get-well cards for Granny, etc.

Storage Box 1	Storage Box 2	Storage Box 3	Storage Box 4
Pens	Paper	Pencils	??
	??		Materials

T
A
B
L
E

Craft area set-up

Each table should seat approximately six children. Three leaders can oversee the whole area (during free play, one staff member should be enough). Ensure that children go to the storage boxes a few at a time. If there are more than 40 children, the rotation plan should be used (as outlined earlier in "Daily Format") if at all possible.

Table 1 – Set Craft	Table 2 – Set Craft	Table 3 – Alternative Craft	Storage Boxes
Table 4 – Main Craft Activity ("Kim's Island")	Table 5 – Set Craft	Table 6 – Free Choice	with craft materials

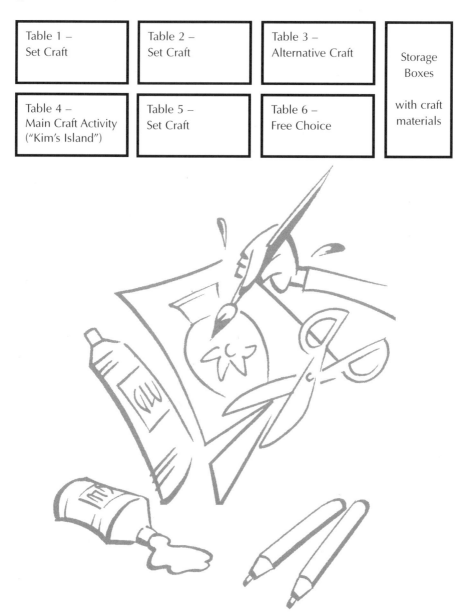

ONGOING CRAFT – KIM'S ISLAND

This is a small-group activity that should last all week. The basic format of the week is:

- **Day 1** Read through the "Kim's Quest" story and design the island.
- **Day 2** Choose the best island design and mark it out on a board base.
- **Day 3** Prepare papier-mâché.
- **Day 4** Paint the island.
- **Day 5** Decorate the island.

Objects needed: *Chicken wire, newspaper, large bowl, glue (PVA), flour, mugs, paints, sand, small branches, kitchen foil.*

Day 1

This is simply a pencil-and-paper exercise. Remember to include the waterfall, the mountain where Jamie and Melanie are trapped, the beach area, the woods, etc. More extravagant attempts may also include the ship on the sea.

Day 2

Having looked through the entries, the next stage is to lay out the island roughly onto a large board – the larger, the better (bearing in mind that the larger is also the more expensive!). First, the general layout of the island should be constructed from various-sized boxes: large ones for large mountains, small ones for lesser slopes, down to the flat surface of the beach.

Day 3

Cover the boxes in chicken wire and prepare your papier-mâché.

NOTE: Some preparation of the papier-mâché is needed beforehand or you will not fit this into your time slot.

The recipe for papier-mâché pulp:

1. Cut or tear the newspaper into 1.5cm squares and pack them tightly into the mug to fill it.
2. Place the mugful of paper into a bowl. Soak the paper in hot water for three hours, then knead it into a pulp with your fingers.
3. Add one tablespoon of PVA glue and one tablespoon of flour (per mug of paper) to the bowl.
4. Mix well with hands. Add more glue if needed, until it feels like squashy clay.
5. Apply over the chicken wire.

Day 4

There are options here. If you are going to use sand for the beach, you can leave this area unpainted. Paint the island using lighter greens at the bottom, and darker greens at the top. Paint the sea.

Day 5

Use the kitchen foil as the basis for your waterfall and pool. PVA the beach area and then place the sand on top. Add the branches to make trees at the necessary places. You could also construct the picnic area where the two friends are trapped.

Use your imagination and add items to the island as you see fit: maybe a tribal village, or a volleyball match on the beach!

DAILY CRAFTS

Many of these crafts are used by permission from the www.dltk-kids.com website.

Day 1: Treasure chest

Objects needed: *An empty tissue box, sugar paper (black, yellow, red), scissors, glue and something to colour with.*

- Cover the tissue box with black paper (all sides). Use enough glue so that when we slit open the box top, the paper will stick.
- Using sharp scissors, cut around three sides of the tissue box, about 2.5cm from the top, so that the treasure chest can open. (Have an adult do this, if necessary.)
- You will need to bend back the cardboard on the remaining attached side, so that the chest opens and closes nicely.
- Glue a piece of yellow or red sugar paper (or use felt or tissue paper) to the inside of the "lid" and chest to resemble a nice velvet lining.
- Photocopy the template from Appendix 2.
- Colour the pieces as necessary and cut them out.
- Glue the KEEP OUT warning onto the top (lid) of the chest.
- Cut 1cm strips from yellow construction paper and glue them to all the edges of the treasure chest.
- Glue the lock onto the front of the chest.
- Glue the handles onto the sides of the chest.
- OPTIONAL: Glue sequins, fake jewels or painted rocks onto the lid to create a jewel-encrusted treasure chest.
- Fill the chest with "topaz", today's precious stone. (Any matching-coloured stones will do.)

Day 2: Friends

Objects needed: *Much paint, lots of paper, a marker pen to write the children's names.*

- If it is possible to do this outside, all the better. In that case you could print feet as well as hands.
- Set out trays of paint and let the children dip their hands in the paint and make handprints on paper. Label each handprint with the child's name.

Day 3: Boats

Objects needed: *Corks, cocktails sticks, thin card, glue, paints.*

- Glue four corks together, side by side, to form the base of the boat.
- Cut the card into triangles as wide as the cork boat.
- Decorate the triangle.
- Cut a tiny cross at the top and bottom of the card.
- Push the cocktail stick through the holes.
- Push the cocktail stick into the cork base, to form a sail.

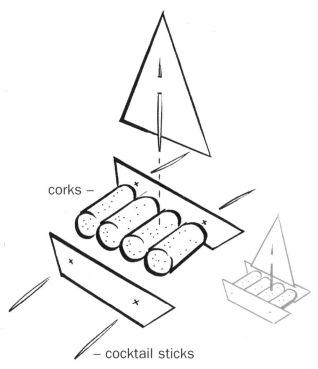

corks –

– cocktail sticks

Day 4: Parrots

Objects needed: *A toilet roll tube, glue, scissors, something to colour with and a piece of paper.*

- Photocopy the template from Appendix 2 onto card.
- Colour the pieces as appropriate and cut them out.
- Glue the large rectangular piece around the toilet paper tube.
- Glue tail onto the back of the toilet roll. (You may want to glue it to the inside back and then fold it upward.)
- Glue the head onto the front of the roll.
- Glue the wings onto the sides of the roll or make it look as if the parrot is flying by gluing the wings onto the back of the roll.
- Fold the feet and glue the tabs to the inside of the tube.

Day 5: Angel pen–holder

Objects needed: *An empty yogurt pot, coloured paper, white paper, cotton-wool balls, black marker pen or paint, hair-coloured wool, scissors, glue.*

- Cover the yogurt pot in coloured paper or white paper and decorate it.
- Photocopy the wings template from Appendix 2.
- Cut out the template pieces.
- Cover these with glue and cover with pieces of cotton wool.
- You can glue the wings onto a piece of cardboard (e.g. from old cereal boxes) before you cut them out, to make them sturdier, if you wish. Glue the wings onto the back of the pot (don't glue them too low – make sure the pot can still stand up properly).
- Take the wool and wrap it around your hand about ten times. Remove the bundle from your hand and tie it at the "top" with a piece of wool.
- Snip the bottom ends so that the wool resembles long hair.
- Glue the "hair" to the side of the angel's head. Make another identical bundle and glue it to the other side of the head.
- Make a third bundle, this time wrapping the wool about 20 times around two fingers instead of your whole hand. Don't tie or snip this bundle. Fluff it out and glue it along the top of the pot.
- Using marker pen or paint, draw a face on the angel.
- Younger children may prefer to glue on wiggly eyes (or make paper eyes with white paper and a marker), a pompom or sequin nose, and a felt or paper mouth, as they won't be able to draw a face very well.

Alternative craft

Each day, have spare paper, colouring pens/pencils, and plenty of colouring books on the alternative craft table.

Take—home activities

WHY TAKE–HOME COMPETITIONS?

The simple answer is that we want to involve the whole family in our activities. For this reason it is often a good idea to send home crosswords; the children will have to ask their parents for help with them. Also, from time to time ask the children a fairly difficult question and promise them bonus points for their team if they come back with the answer the next day. I have seen children phoning uncles and grandparents in their desperation to find the answers to such questions as these:

- Who invented the light bulb?
- Where was Mother Teresa born?
- What is the fourteenth book of the Old Testament?
- Who framed Roger Rabbit?

The Friday take-home activity is particularly important because it contains the invitation to the Sunday service as well as the colouring competition itself. The five-day take-home material includes:

- **Day 1** Wordsearch
- **Day 2** Quiz
- **Day 3** Crossword
- **Day 4** Match
- **Day 5** Colouring competition (and invitation to all-age worship) shown in Appendix 1.

Day 1: Wordsearch

A	C	F	W	R	T	Y	U	I	K	J	H	G	F	D	S
Y	S	T	I	A	E	T	O	P	L	M	N	C	D	F	G
T	F	E	F	E	I	R	E	X	O	R	P	H	Y	O	G
R	G	K	I	M	B	E	R	L	Y	Y	Z	E	B	N	M
E	H	G	G	E	D	A	F	Y	T	Q	Z	S	B	M	L
Q	J	H	R	R	V	S	K	J	H	G	D	T	E	W	A
U	K	J	R	A	O	U	B	M	C	A	Z	S	G	H	O
E	L	I	O	L	Q	R	X	B	M	M	N	A	E	W	A
S	M	V	C	D	Q	E	F	U	Y	I	O	G	G	T	H
T	D	R	Y	I	P	R	W	C	F	J	L	M	E	Q	D
U	E	Q	S	V	B	M	J	U	I	S	H	T	R	L	E
A	T	T	I	C	Y	B	N	M	C	H	W	Z	X	Q	P
S	Y	W	H	P	A	T	R	E	W	I	Z	X	C	V	N
A	N	M	J	H	G	E	W	Q	Y	P	O	P	M	B	V
V	B	N	M	P	Q	W	E	R	T	Y	U	H	G	F	S

Treasure

Chest

Emerald

Attic

Ship

Angel

Quest

Kim

Day 2: Quiz

1. What is the name of the main character in our story? **Kim**
2. What are her friends called? **Mel (Melanie) and Jamie**
3. What is the first book in the Bible? **Genesis**
4. Which football team are nicknamed "the gunners"? **Arsenal**
5. What colour do you get when you mix red and blue? **Purple**
6. What is the fourth planet from the sun? **Mars**
7. Who was the Road Runner escaping from? **Wile E. Coyote**
8. Who invented the light bulb? **Thomas Edison**
9. What colour is amethyst? **Purple**
10. What basketball player featured in *Space Jam*?
    Michael Jordan

Day 3: Crossword

Across

1. The _____ of greatest worth.
3. Planet Kim is trying to save.
5. Asil is one.
6. Longer version of our heroine's name.
10. Like a hare.

Down

1. The first special stone.
2. The second special stone.
4. To do with the past.
7. One of Kim's friends.
8. Special time when we celebrate Jesus' death and resurrection.
9. Another of Kim's friends.

Day 4: Match

Match the following with their homes:

Day 5: Colouring competition

This activity (full size) is in the handout section, Appendix 1.

Choosing videos

HOW TO WATCH. WHERE TO WATCH. WHAT TO WATCH.

How to watch.

No matter how good the choice of video, there will always be at least one child who hasn't quite got the hang of sitting still. Give an incentive. The child who sits the best receives a small prize. This may seem like bribery – it is! However, in this context the needs of the many certainly outweigh the needs of the few. The whole video session could become disrupted because of one or two unruly children.

In the worst-case scenario, a problem child may need to be removed from the video session and sent to sit in a quiet area to read a book for five minutes.

Where to watch.

You may be amazed by how small an area you actually need for the video session. However, it is clear that larger television screens help. Those groups with video projectors come into their own at this point.

Children seem to prefer sitting on the floor; a few bean bags scattered around aid the whole process. Dim the lights and enjoy!

If large numbers of children mean that you are operating with three groups rotating between the activity sections, then your video area could be a spare classroom, a corner of the main hall, a corridor – we have used all of these and they all work perfectly well.

What to watch.

This is where it gets a little more difficult. What you ultimately watch will boil down to personal taste; the following is for guidance only and is based on our experience.

There is one clear fact: you only have 30 minutes of viewing time. This is not particularly restricting – it means you can watch a feature-length movie over several days or you can watch several 30-minute videos. So what can you watch?

Veggie Tales: These are excellent animation-style videos. Each video contains good, solid moral and spiritual teaching, usually based on a Biblical narrative. Children from Christian homes respond very well to this video series (there are now more than enough videos in this series to get you through the week). The younger the children, the better they like it. However, children from non-Christian homes don't respond so well and often dislike these videos. The other negative is that the stories are based on Bible stories and sometimes this makes Bible teaching a little more difficult.

Testament: This series of videos produced by the Bible Society is excellent. In my experience children from both Christian and non-Christian homes enjoy watching these videos. I never cease to be amazed by how little of the narrative the children know. This post-Christian generation doesn't know its Bible stories.

Story Keepers: This is another great series, in which children travel back in time and view some very exciting Bible stories first-hand. Apart from the presence of the "time travellers", the Bible stories are very accurate.

Penguins: From the same stable as *Veggie Tales*. This is another excellently produced series but, again, non-Christian children are less excited by it.

There are many other choices. You may be amazed by how much your local Christian bookshop manager knows! Also, he or she will inevitably have received feedback.

Feature-length videos

Miracle Maker: This is an amazing production by the Bible Society. I can't think of one negative comment to make on it.

Secular videos: The Disney movies and those who follow their style certainly keep children from multiple backgrounds engaged. There are some points to make in thinking through your choice:

- Do you really want to miss the opportunity for clear Christian input by taking the easier option and showing a familiar Disney movie?
- Many Disney movies carry unclear spiritual messages. The "circle of life" motif in *The Lion King* is not a Christian concept. *Pocahontas* involves spirits in the forest, which may also cause some difficulty! There are plenty of other examples. View with a discerning mindset.

There are, however, plenty of secular movies which are excellent, e.g. *Toy Story*, *Chicken Run*, *The Fox and the Hound*, and of course the legendary *Wallace and Gromit* films, which in my experience have never failed to engage the audience.

My recommendation for this week:

Monday:	*Wallace and Gromit: The Wrong Trousers*
Tuesday:	*Miracle Maker* (first 30 minutes)
Wednesday:	*Miracle Maker* (second 30 minutes)
Thursday:	*Miracle Maker* (final 30 minutes)
Friday:	*Wallace and Gromit: A Grand Day Out*

Ideas for outside games

OUTSIDE GAMES AND ALTERNATIVES

There is a wide range of games available for this activity slot; most Guide or Scout leaders will be able to recommend many games. Several are listed below, but it is also important to have alternative activities. Not every child likes playing games. You could perhaps have a face-painting session at the same time as games (it's easier than you would think – but also remember you need parental permission before you do it) or allow an extra craft activity.

It is also worth remembering that on some of the days you could simply walk the children to the local park for this slot. This may seem a little uneventful, but the children enjoy being there in large numbers.

Welly throwing

Objects needed: *Several old wellies, several hoops or tyres, pieces of chalk.*

1. Chalk a number, e.g. 10, 50, 80, 100, on the side of the tyres or in the middle of the hoops.
2. The children line up one behind the other at a set point.
3. Each player stands at a set point and throws his or her welly towards the hoops/tyres. Each player's score is recorded. Once they have thrown, they return to the back of the line.
4. At the end of the session the scores are added up.

Assault course

Objects needed: *Tyres, buckets, balls, sacks, eggs, a board, several bricks and spoons.*

1. The children line up one behind the other at a set point.
2. The children set off through the assault course, 20 seconds apart. They may go several times. Have the children...
   a) climb through a hanging tyre.
   b) crawl through a standing tyre.
   c) throw balls into a bucket from a set distance.
   d) run along a board supported by bricks.
   e) jump along in a sack.
   f) run with an egg and spoon over a set distance.

g) do a "roly-poly" to finish.
3. The quickest time wins. Give prizes for first, second and third place.

Funny football

Objects needed: *Two footballs, markers to make two goals.*

1. The pitch is set up as a standard football pitch.
2. The players are split evenly.
3. This is exactly the same as normal football, but you use two balls!
4. If this is not strange enough, add two more goals so that you have four goals making a diamond shape, or have four teams and three balls!

Quick cricket

Objects needed: *One set of cricket stumps, a marker five metres from the cricket stumps to the side and a marker five metres ahead where the bowler stands, a cricket bat (or tennis bat) and balls.*

1. All the children are fielders except for one batter. The leader bowls.
2. The ball is bowled (underarm). If the ball is hit or missed, the batter must run to the five-metre marker and back again.
3. The fielders try to get the ball back to the bowler as fast as possible.

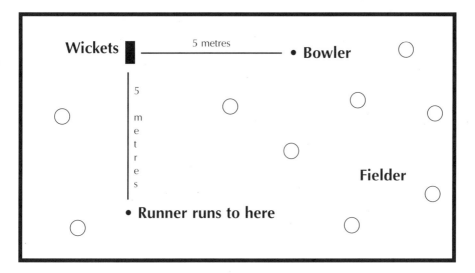

4. The bowler does not wait until the ball returns before he or she bowls again.
5. When the ball eventually hits the wicket, the batter changes.
6. A record is kept of the number of runs for each player.
7. The winner, obviously, is the player with the most runs.

Bulldog

Object needed: *A ball (in some versions of the game only).*

There are many variations and titles for this game. The basic version works like this:

1. All the children except two stand at one end of the playing area. The remaining two children stand in the middle.
2. The children in the middle say a certain word – in this case, "bulldog".
3. The other children must not move until they hear this word; when they do, they must run from one side of the playing area to the other, without getting caught.
4. The players in the middle try to catch them – to successfully catch them they must get hold of them and count to ten. Alternatives involve just touching them.
5. When a player is caught, he or she joins those in the centre; the other children – on hearing the word "bulldog" – have to get back.
6. When all the children are caught, the first two caught stand in the middle and the game begins again.

Another version involves those in the middle throwing balls (below the waist) at those who are running. Those hit by the ball join the children in the middle. Obviously, be careful not to allow play to get too rough; this game is not particularly suitable for children under eight years old.

Parachute games

Objects needed: *A parachute, a ball.*

There are many books that show a variety of parachute games. These are excellent. Parachutes are relatively cheap, and it is actually possible with the right degree of charm to get old parachutes from the RAF and Army – give them a call. If you have a small group, the parachutes that you can purchase from most toy magazines will be fine. The military parachutes really come into their own with larger groups.

Outside games for week:

	Activity
Monday	
Tuesday	
Wednesday	
Thursday	
Friday	

Afternoon activities

WHY AND WHAT AFTERNOON ACTIVITIES?

Why afternoon activities?

It is possible to run a perfectly good holiday club that ends after (or before) lunch, without the need for afternoon activities. However, to do this misses out on one of the most important principles of our work with children: if we don't have fun with them, they will not listen to us.

We have proved this again and again. Children who had no intention of listening to us during the first day became the most attentive listeners the day after a swimming session together, or after ice skating at the local rink.

What afternoon activities?

All the activities have negative and positive aspects, but as a baseline guide, ensure plenty of variety and note well the safety comments listed. Choose five activities that enhance your week without blowing your budget. Take note of the activities available in your area.

You will need parental permission for practically everything you do. If you are doing face-painting, parents will usually have to sign a form ahead of time giving permission for this. If you intend to go on an outing, you will be committing an offence if you take any child outside your building without a signed consent form from the parents. These rules and regulations shouldn't stop us doing fun and wholesome activities, but we do need to think through all the implications before we go ahead.

If you take your children on an outing, the relevant authorities will expect you to have done a risk assessment and to have taken any necessary measures to reduce the risk.

Swimming

A proper pool with qualified lifeguards is essential; never take shortcuts when safety is an issue.

Advantages

- This activity should be relatively inexpensive.
- It is great for getting to know the children.

- As long as the pool has the appropriate shallow and deep ends, children of differing ages and abilities can enjoy the same activity together.

Disadvantages

- In my limited lifetime I suspect we have lost enough clothes during our swimming sessions to smartly dress a small nation.
- If something goes wrong in the other activities the worst that can happen is usually a broken bone – here the consequences could be far more serious.
- Some pools will ask for ratios of one adult to every two or three children; this is often impossible for larger groups.

Ice / Roller skating

Advantages

- It is great to be able to teach children new things. Some of the children will never have done these activities before and will need step-by-step tuition – this is great relationship-building.
- It is great to hear children running out to their parents proclaiming: "Mum, I can ice skate!"

Disadvantages

- At last count, I have spent roughly half my life tying shoe laces for ice or roller skating (that was hyperbole – but it does feel like it sometimes).
- It can get quite exhausting for your leaders to spend all their time trying to teach the children who have never been ice or roller skating before.
- Accidents can occur.

Children's activity centres

Advantages

- Children of many ages can enjoy a wide variety of specially designed activities at the same time, from slides to ball pools to ropes.
- These are usually reasonably priced.

Disadvantages

- These centres are very popular, so the owners may be reluctant to admit a large group or give a group discount.

Nature treks

Advantages

- These are great activities for the summer. You will need to have a list of items that the children have to:

  a) collect (twig, pine cone, feather, etc.) OR
  b) see (river, bird, sheep, etc.).

Disadvantages

- Rain! Although children (and I) usually like walking in the rain, often parents seem to have a problem with it!

Ten-pin bowling

Advantages

- Because of the guides that can be put up and the special rolling machine, all ages can enjoy this activity.

Disadvantages

- It can finish very quickly.
- It can take as much time to enter everyone's names as it does to play the game.
- Supervision of wandering children is quite difficult.

Inflatable afternoon

Maybe the answer is not to go off site but to hire a load of inflatables in. You can now hire Sumo suits and inflatable assault courses as well as the traditional bouncy castle.

Advantages

- This really is a lot of fun.

Disadvantages

- Children can get hurt easily, especially if the castles are not supervised properly.
- There may be implications for your insurance.
- Rain!

Sports day

- You will need to think up eight different activities for the children, e.g. they have to carry table-tennis balls from one bucket of water to the other, using their toes, or dribble a football between the cones and back again. One base can be for juice. Set up eight bases in the playing area (see diagram below).
- Each base will need a leader.
- You will then need to split the children into eight groups.
- The children will do each of the activities for ten minutes. The score for the group will then be recorded.
- The leader will stand in the middle to start the ten minutes and end the ten minutes. He or she will also give the command to run to the next activity.
- At the end of the day, the scores are added and the winning team found.
- The set-up of the area should look like this:

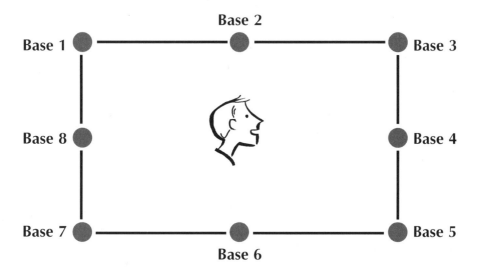

Base 1 — Base 2 — Base 3
Base 8 — Base 4
Base 7 — Base 6 — Base 5

Advantages

- This is very cost-effective and a lot of fun – particularly if lots of bases have a water-based activity.

Disadvantages

- You need lots of leaders to make it run smoothly.

Cinema / theatre

Advantages

- A potentially good two-hour activity.

Disadvantages

- It is hard to find the right movie, especially one that the children haven't seen before. This is less of a problem in the case of the theatre.
- It could be expensive.

Day trips (seaside, theme parks, safari parks, zoos)

Advantages

- It becomes a whole-day activity.
- It is usually very enjoyable.

Disadvantages

- It is expensive.
- The seaside seems designed to be dangerous!

Afternoon activities for week:

	Activity
Monday	
Tuesday	
Wednesday	
Thursday	
Friday	

Format for all-age worship service

ALL-AGE WORSHIP SERVICE FORMAT

Many ministers approach the idea of the all-age worship service with great trepidation. It is true to say that if done badly, the all-age service is a nightmare; if done well, it is an excellent outreach tool. The format suggested here is simply to point you in the right direction for the all-age service which immediately follows your Bible club week.

Arrival

Ensure that there is some good background music playing – it can be quite intimidating to walk in to silence – and that a familiar face from the Bible club is standing at the door. Those at the door are doing three things:

- welcoming people
- collecting completed colouring competition entries
- showing people to suitable seats.

Welcome

At the start of the service, welcome everyone but make a special effort to make the parents of the children who attended the Bible club welcome and comfortable. You could say a few words as follows:

"Good morning and welcome! A special welcome to all those children and parents of the children who attended the Bible club last week; I have heard it was a great success. We will be judging the colouring competitions a little later and we hope you can stay with us for teas and coffees at the end. This morning we will be singing some songs, many of which will have actions, and there will also be some drama and a puppet show. And there will be a short time of prayer. Please relax and enjoy the service."

Items

Be courageous and use a lot of variety. You are aiming for a service lasting an hour. The preaching time will take 20 minutes of this, so also use action songs, ordinary songs, prayer time, drama and maybe even a brief puppet show. Try and tie them to the theme used in the story below.

Preaching

Some of the people who attend may never do so again, so you will want to present the gospel. However, if you present it too strongly, you can guarantee they will never attend again. I suggest the story that follows:

> George was born in the State of Georgia in the United States of America. His parents lived on a plantation. The house they lived in belonged to a very wealthy man indeed and they worked for that man and he paid them for their work. They in turn paid rent to that man to live in the house. It was hard work; they got up every morning at sunrise, and went out into the fields to plant or to dig or to gather in the crops. They worked through until sunset and then returned home to make dinner. George's mother and father both worked in the fields and, come harvest time, George would help out as well. The people didn't mind working because the owner of the land paid them quite well. The pay was not brilliant, but good enough to pay their rent, buy food and clothes, and sometimes even to buy chocolate.
>
> It hadn't always been this way. George's grandfather had worked the same land but as a slave. He had been treated very poorly and was forced to work very hard with no pay at all.
>
> George's mother and father couldn't read. But George knew that if he wanted to do what was in his heart to do, then he would have to learn to read. He began to teach himself and, with just a little help from the rich man's daughter, who went to a nearby school, he learned to read. But he wanted to do more than read; he wanted to go to Princeton College – a very famous college – where he wanted to train to become a lawyer. But Princeton cost many thousands of dollars to attend even back then and George's mum and dad would never have enough money to send him.
>
> George's mum and dad tried to convince him that it was impossible, but he refused to believe them. He was determined. He knew he would never get enough money to go to Princeton by staying on the plantation so he headed for the city and eventually got a job as a porter on a train. He would carry suitcases on and off the train, collect tickets, show people to their seats – he would do anything to earn more

money to pay for his fees for when he eventually got to Princeton.

One of the things he would do to try and earn a little more money was to stay up into the early hours of the morning, cleaning and polishing people's shoes. He would knock on the doors of the passengers – for George worked on a long-distance train with bedrooms built in – and ask if they needed their shoes polishing. He would then work late into the night polishing shoes. At 1am, 2am, 3am, 4am he would be up cleaning and polishing shoes – it may sound an easy job but scraping doggy do-do off shoes into the middle of the morning was not George's idea of fun. Still, he wanted to go to Princeton and nothing was going to stop him. And then at 7am every morning, he would get up and begin his portering work. He worked very hard.

Mr Spencer was a businessman. He travelled on the train very often. But on this particular night he had a lot on his mind – he'd just started a business deal in Chicago and was on his way to New York to complete another deal. His mind was working very quickly. It was 2am and he couldn't sleep, so he decided to go for a walk. He made his way along the train and then he saw a light on in the engine room. He walked up and looked in. There, sitting on the floor, was George, surrounded by hundreds of pairs of shoes.

George looked up as Mr Spencer walked in: "Good evening, sir, or should I say, good morning? What brings you up here?"

Mr Spencer explained that he couldn't sleep. He then enquired what George was doing and, more to the point, why. George made Mr Spencer a milky drink and began to explain how he was working so very hard to go to Princeton to train to be a lawyer. Mr Spencer listened intently before he returned to his carriage to go to sleep. That was the last George saw of Mr Spencer.

George worked for another year on that train until eventually he had enough money to pay for the first term's fees at Princeton. There was no way he could get all the money, but he had enough for the first term. He made an appointment with the headmaster of Princeton College and went to see him.

Most people would have given up many years earlier. Many would never have started. But George knew what he wanted to do and wasn't going to let anyone stop him. It may have seemed impossible but here he was in the office of the headmaster of Princeton College.

"You've sent me some money, George," the headmaster began, "but I can't take it."

George began to shake. Had he worked so hard and so long and still he wouldn't be allowed to enter the college? He tried to explain: "Mr Headmaster, I know the money's not enough for three years; I know it's not enough for one year; but if you could just let me pay for the first term, then I will go away and earn enough money for the second term and come back again, and then go and earn enough for the third. But please let me start, I've worked so hard... "

The headmaster smiled. "George, I didn't mean you couldn't attend. I meant I couldn't take your money. A year ago, a man called Mr Spencer walked into this office and handed me enough money for you to stay in college for three years – until the end of the course – but he said this to me... He said that you were only to have the money if you actually came."

Many people think coming to God is impossible. They think that they will never make it, that they will never be good enough, or righteous enough. They are absolutely right. In our own strength we cannot come to God. But in the same way that George could never have entered Princeton without the help of a man with great resources, we too have a great Benefactor. He has available to him the entire resources of heaven. He came, he lived amongst us, he died on a cross to make heaven accessible to you and me, to make God accessible to you and me. We could not do it; he did it for us. We could never be good enough, but when we give our lives to Jesus, it is as if we are wrapped in Jesus and when God looks at us he sees Jesus. We are clothed in righteousness.

Ladies and gentlemen, if you are willing, you can approach God today through Jesus. God is willing. There will be opportunity for prayer after the meeting.

So George began his course and four years later he became a lawyer. Some time after that he became a high court judge, one of the first black men in the USA to do so. Because he tried.

Conclusion

- Give the prize for the best entry in the colouring competition.
- Remind people of the opportunity for prayer that is available.
- Invite everyone to stay for teas and coffees.
- Make sure there is plenty of literature about regarding upcoming services, Alpha/Emmaus courses, etc.

APPENDIX 1
Handouts

SAMPLE LEAFLET

Sample leaflet to advertise your children's club

KIM'S QUEST COLOURING COMPETITION AND INVITATION TO ALL-AGE WORSHIP

Name: _____

The best colouring handed in at Sunday's all-age service will win a prize

St Mary's invites you to an

ALL-AGE SERVICE

ST MARY's CHURCH
Rickley Lane, Bletchley

This Sunday 10–11:15am

Join us for refreshments afterwards
Further information on (01908) 000000

Sample all-age worship invitation to go on back of
colouring competition

Further Information From:

Church Office
?????
?????
?????

Tel. (01908) 000000
Fax: (01908) 000000

Other projects include:

1. FRANTIC: children's club
2. GAMES ZONE
3. HOLIDAY PLAYSCHEMES
4. BREAKFAST CLUBS
5. SUMMER CAMP
6. X-TREME YOUTH CLUB (11–16)
7. BREAKOUT

Please telephone for further details

Terms and Conditions

1. Playscheme payment must arrive at least two weeks before the event or your place will be reissued to people on the waiting list.

2. We reserve the right to refuse registration, or cancel registration, to children with persistent discipline problems.

3. While every effort will be made to safeguard your child's possessions whilst they are with us, no responsibility can be taken for loss or damage of property.

4. No person other than those authorised in writing by the parent/guardian will be allowed to pick up your children.

Kim's Quest
THE HOLIDAY
PLAYSCHEME

WITH TRIPS TO
KIDS WORLD &
MEGA BOWL

August
15th to 22nd

St Mary's Church Hall
BLETCHLEY

Monday to Friday
8:30–5:45pm

Dear Parent,

There are various reasons why you may need the resource of a holiday playscheme. You may be a working parent and want to be sure your child is in a safe and secure environment. You may simply need some extra space during the holidays. Whatever the reason, we believe that our holiday playschemes can meet your needs and the needs of your child(ren).

We are also aware of the strains on the budget of the modern family, so we have endeavoured to provide the service for the best possible price. We are able to look after your child in a spacious, well-equipped environment with excellent staff for an incredibly reasonable price.

The weekly rate is £40.00 and the daily rate is £10. If you have any further queries please contact me.
Mark Griffiths

ACTIVITIES

We have a wide range of activities available. The morning will consist of indoor activities such as games, quizzes, stories, crafts, videos, competitions, songs, etc. During the afternoon the children choose between the following options:

AFTERNOON ACTIVITIES

Monday	Cinema
Tuesday	Swimming
Wednesday	Ten-pin bowling
Thursday	Nature trek
Friday	Kids World

All activities are included in the registration price.

ARRIVAL & DEPARTURE

Parents dropping off children may do so between 8:30am and 10:00am and should collect them between 4pm and 5:45pm.

SAFETY & STAFFING

The safety and wellbeing of the child is our first concern. We maintain a ratio of 1 staff member to every 8 children (1:10 for over-8s) and have a first-aider on site at all times. We ensure that all our staff are police-checked. For safety reasons we have restricted attendance.

REGISTRATION

If you would like your child to be a part of this Fusion project, please complete the registration form opposite and return it direct to us by post with full payment. We will confirm your place by post within 14 days, along with any additional information you may require. Places are limited and will be issued on a 'first come, first served' basis.

PROGRAMME

We run an exciting and innovative programme involving seven distinct zones.

Zone 1:	Library/Homework corner
2:	Arts & crafts (varies daily)
3:	Chat back
4:	Computer games
5:	Pool, snooker or table tennis
6:	Children's television, video days
7:	Outside play: basketball, etc.
8:	Video days

THE USUAL FORMAT OF PLAYSCHEMES IS:

8:30–10:00am	Drop off and free play
10:00–11:00am	Talk time*
11:00–11:15pm	Biscuits and juice
11:15–12:00noon	Outside games
12:00–12:45pm	Video
12:45–1:15pm	Lunch**
1:15–2:00pm	Craft
2:00–4:00pm	Afternoon activities
4:00–4:15pm	Biscuits and juice
4:30–5:45pm	Collections and free play

WE LEAVE FOR AFTERNOON ACTIVITIES AT 12:30 ON WEDNESDAY AND FRIDAY.

* Talk time involves discussion of Christian values such as truth, honesty, fairness, etc.
** A packed lunch will be needed. Drinks and biscuits are given in the morning and afternoon.

FINAL COMMENT

We have endeavoured to make sure our holiday playscheme provision is of the highest standard. Along with our after-schools projects we run child care to the degree of excellence that your child/ren deserve. We are committed to providing affordable, quality child care.

REGISTRATION FORM

Child's Name: _____

Address: _____

Tel: _____ Child's D.o.B.: _____

School Attended: _____

Medical Conditions/Food Allergies we should be aware of:
_____

In the event of a major accident, your child will be taken, by ambulance if possible, to the nearest casualty department and parents will be informed as soon as possible. If this is not the procedure you would like us to follow for your child, please notify us in writing before your child starts.

Signed: _____

_____ Date: _____

Payment must be received within two weeks of the playscheme or we will reissue the place. Please make cheques payable to ????

APPENDIX 2
Craft
Templates

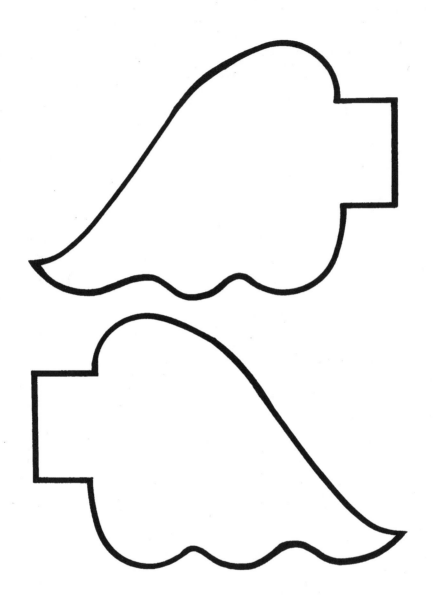

APPENDIX 3
Bible Texts

"I will bless you with a future filled with hope – a future of success."

Jeremiah 29:11

"If we cannot forgive those who sin against us, God will not forgive us."

Matthew 18:35

"God cares for you, so turn all your worries over to him."

1 Peter 5:7

"When you stood at the crossroads, I [God] told you, 'Follow the road your ancestors took, and you will find peace.'"

Jeremiah 6:16

"Jesus wept."

John 11:35

APPENDIX 4
Resources

RECOMMENDED RESOURCES

MUSIC

Children of the Cross, Jim Bailey (Kingsway)
God's Gang, Jim Bailey (Kingsway)
King of Heaven, Doug Horley (Kingsway)
Shout to the Lord Kids! 1 & 2, North Point Church (Integrity)
Whoopah Wahey!, Doug Horley (Kingsway)
Lovely Jubbly, Doug Horley (Kingsway)
Ishmael's Collections, Ishmael (Kingsway)
Soul Survivor Collections, Compilation (Survivor Records)
Extreme Worship, Jim Bailey (Kingsway)

BOOKS

77 Talks for 21st Century Kids, Chris Chesterton (Monarch)
52 Ideas for Junior Classroom Assemblies, Chris Chesterton and Pat Gutteridge (Monarch)
52 Ideas for Infant School Assemblies, Chris Chesterton and Elaine Buckley (Monarch)
77 Talks for Cyberspace Kids, Chris Chesterton and David T. Ward (Monarch)
Fusion, Mark Griffiths (Monarch)
Impact, Mark Griffiths (Monarch)
Don't Tell Cute Stories – Change Lives, Mark Griffiths (Monarch)
Reclaiming a Generation, Ishmael (Kingsway)
Devil Take the Youngest, Winkie Pratney (Bethany House)
Fire on the Horizon, Winkie Pratney (Renew Books, Gospel Light)
Streets of Pain, Bill Wilson (Word)
A Theology of Children's Ministry, Lawrence O. Richards (Zondervan)
The Prayer of Jabez for Kids, Bruce Wilkinson (Tommy Nelson Inc)
Come Holy Spirit, David Pytches (Hodder & Stoughton)

VIDEOS

The Veggie Tales Series, Big Idea Productions (distr. Word)
The Testament Series (Bible Society)
Miracle Maker (Bible Society)
Story Keepers (Zondervan/20th Century Fox)

RECOMMENDED WEBSITES FOR RESOURCE MATERIAL

www.kingdomcreative.co.uk
www.ishmael.org.uk
www.jubilee-kids.org
www.armslength.com

www.duggiedugdug.co.uk
www.kidzblitz.com
www.tricksfortruth.com

PUPPETS AND GENERAL

For a spectacular range of puppets, visit www.armslength.com or www.tricksfortruth.com

SUMMER CAMPS

For information on interdenominational summer camps for children, check out www.treasurekids.co.uk

FOR OTHER CRAFT ACTIVITIES

www.dltk-kids.com

SHORT-TERM MISSION

Kings Kids offer short-term mission opportunities for children and can be contacted via the Youth With A Mission website, www.ywam.org

TRAINING CHILDREN'S LEADERS

For annual training events for children's leaders, please check out www.new-wine.org

CONTACT

If you would like Mark Griffiths to come and talk to your children's leaders, or you have any observations to make on this book, please contact me on markgriff@lineone.net